More Than Magnets

Exploring the Wonders of Science in Preschool and Kindergarten

by
Sally Moomaw
and
Brenda Hieronymus

Redleaf Press

Published by: Redleaf Press
                a division of Resources for Child Caring
                450 N. Syndicate, Suite 5
                St. Paul, MN 55104

Moomaw, Sally, 1948-
    More than magnets : exploring the wonders of science in preschool
and kindergarten / by Sally Moomaw and Brenda Hieronymus.
        p.   cm.
    ISBN 1-884834-33-7 (alk. paper)
    1. Science--Study and teaching (Preschool) 2. Education,
Preschool--Activity programs. 3. Interdisciplinary approach in
education. I. Hieronymus, Brenda, 1945- . II. Title.
LB1140.5.S35M66   1997   97-23247
                                                CIP

For Peter, Jeffrey, and Charlie

—Sally Moomaw

For Claire and Bob

—Brenda Hieronymus

Acknowledgments

We would like to thank Charles Moomaw for his assistance throughout the preparation of this book. His help at each phase of the process was invaluable.

We are indebted to Peter Moomaw and Karen Hersman for helping us phrase scientific information simply yet accurately. They also supplied background information on scientific principles.

We also thank David C. Baxter of PhotoGraphic Services, University of Cincinnati, for the endless hours he spent working with us on this project. David's enthusiasm was inspiring. He was always willing to take "one last photo" or organize one more group of children.

We appreciate the support of our colleagues at the Arlitt Child and Family Research and Education Center, University of Cincinnati. Facilities, equipment, and materials from the center were used in some of the photographs in the book.

A special thanks goes to the children who participated in the photo sessions: Alice, Allison, Aloke, Andrew, Angki, Anna, Anne, Ayan, Ayanna, Bonnie, Brandon, Brian, Bryant, Charles, Daniel, David, Diamond, Elijah, Emily, Evan, Fumimaro, Jennie, Jonathan, Joshua, Kaitlin, Kollijanni, Kristilyn, Loren, Lori, Mengyue, Nicholas, Preeya, Saahil, Sammy, Samudra, Shelly, Simone, Sumedha, Tiffany, Tracey, Trevor, and Tyler.

Contents

Chapter 4 Science in the Sensory Table 97

Chapter 7 Science in Cooking 241

Chapter 8 Science in Gross-Motor Areas 269

Appendix

Preface

Early childhood teachers, caregivers, and parents are aware of the tremendous interest young children have in exploring their world, figuring out how things work, and experimenting with new materials. At heart, every young child is a scientist seeking explanations for each new phenomenon. Yet science curriculums typically do not capitalize on the hands-on, self-initiated learning style of young children. Curriculum guides often emphasize teacher-directed experiments or the memorization of facts, and they tend to concentrate on the life sciences (plants and animals). Few address physics and chemistry for young children. This leaves teachers and parents searching for ways to stimulate scientific thinking and learning in young children. *More Than Magnets: Exploring the Wonders of Science in Preschool and Kindergarten* fills the need for a comprehensive, developmentally appropriate approach to science education with young children, with special attention to physics and chemistry.

Science opportunities exist in all areas of the classroom; however, teachers are sometimes unaware that science can be explored throughout the curriculum. They often question how to guide children in the discovery of scientific knowledge. *More Than Magnets* contains more than a hundred activities that engage children in interactive science explorations in many areas of the classroom. An introductory chapter is followed by chapters on science displays, machines and pendulums, science in the sensory table, art activities that incorporate science, music and science, exploring science through cooking activities, and science in the gross-motor arena.

Each chapter starts with a section that provides answers to questions teachers and parents commonly ask. This question and answer section is followed by numerous activities that encourage children to explore materials, hypothesize, experiment, and make observations. Each activity is accompanied by a photograph and a description of how to set up the activity or construct the materials. Teachers will find a suggested sequence of implementation so they can start activities simply and build on the children's experiences. Each activity also contains a section called "What to Look For" that guides teachers as they observe children interacting with the materials. Suggestions for questions to extend children's thinking accompany each activity. Since science is part of an integrated learning environment, ideas for related curriculum activities are also included.

Although many teachers and parents are interested in exploring science with young children, some adults may not feel confident in their own scientific knowledge. For this reason, a brief section on related scientific information appears with each activity. This information is not intended as "facts" to "teach" children. Instead, teachers can more easily formulate questions to expand thinking when they understand the science embedded in each activity. In some cases the scientific information provides appropriate vocabulary for teachers to use as they interact with children. In a few instances, especially in chapter 2 ("Science Displays"), the scientific information is appropriate to tell children directly. For example, some animals eat pine nuts, or shells are the homes for some animals. Answers to science-related questions are also discussed in the "Teachers' Questions" section of each chapter.

All of the activities that appear in *More Than Magnets* have been field tested in classrooms at the Arlitt Child and Family Research and Education Center at the University of Cincinnati. The children at the center range in age from three to six years and come from diverse family backgrounds. Some are funded by Head Start, while others pay tuition. Some children have disabilities. The children represent many different cultures and nationalities and speak many different languages. All of the children, both girls and boys, share an excitement for science and find ways to communicate their enthusiasm as they explore the many possibilities presented in their classrooms.

The activities in this book are designed for preschool and kindergarten children. Some of the materials contain small objects. If teachers of younger children wish to adapt some of these activities, they should be certain to use objects that young children cannot swallow.

Science surrounds all of us. May teachers, parents, and children all enjoy exploring its many facets through the activities included in this book.

Introduction to Whole Science

Take a walk through a science-rich early childhood classroom. What might you see?

▲ In the sensory table, children pour a mixture of cornmeal and rice into colanders and watch to see which materials fall through the holes.

▲ In the art area, two children sprinkle glitter onto their paper and are surprised when it doesn't stick. A third child suggests that they need to use glue to hold the glitter.

▲ In the manipulative area, two children build a marble track and try to figure out why the marbles never hit one of the ramps on their structure.

▲ In the science area, children use tweezers to pluck seeds from a sunflower.

▲ At the special activity table, children take turns swinging a pendulum that is dripping paint. They watch in fascination as an elliptical pattern emerges.

All of these children are engaged in scientific exploration. They are constructing important knowledge about the physical properties of materials. In a science-rich environment, science permeates all areas of the classroom. Science is not relegated to an occasional experiment, activity, or field trip. Instead, children are encouraged to explore new materials as a scientist would— forming hypotheses, trying things out, and observing the results. Science is exciting. It intersects with activities all day. We call this *whole science*.

The Whole-Science Classroom
What is whole science?

It is an approach to science education that recognizes that science cannot be separated from other areas of the curriculum or from children's everyday life experiences. Every area of the classroom is filled with potential for scientific learning. A whole-science classroom invites children to explore materials and become keen observers. Through their daily explorations, children construct an understanding of the science concepts that educators have often sought, without much success, to teach from books.

What constitutes a science-rich classroom?

A science-rich classroom conveys an atmosphere that encourages children to explore the scientific properties of materials in all areas of the classroom. Scientific learning is more complete and has greater depth when teachers capitalize on the connections between science and other areas of the curriculum. Unique opportunities for the construction of scientific knowledge emerge in various areas of the classroom:

▲ *Art Area*—Children have many opportunities to observe changes in art materials, such as how the adhesion capabilities of glue emerge as it dries. Art activities also allow children to explore new aspects related to the movement of objects, such as blowing air through a straw to move paint across a paper.

▲ *Sensory Table*—The sensory table allows children to physically explore both liquid and dry materials. They can experiment with how these materials react with other objects or tools. For example, corks can be buried under sand and they stay put, but they repeatedly rise to the top of water.

▲ *Music Area*—The music area provides unique opportunities for children to explore the science of sound. They learn that size affects an instrument's pitch (how high or low it sounds), as when they compare two sizes of triangles. Children also explore the relationship between the material used to make an instrument and its tone quality.

▲ *Cooking*—Through cooking activities children can experiment with simple machines and also observe changes in materials as they react to heat or cold or as they combine with other substances. For example, they might use an egg-beater (wheel and axle) or spoon (lever) to scramble eggs and watch the eggs change form as they are heated.

▲ **Gross-Motor**—Gross-motor activities enable children to experience physical phenomena and simple machines through their entire bodies. For example, riding a teeter-totter gives children a new perspective on weight, balance, and the function of a lever. Many children wait expectantly for the teeter-totter to magically resume motion when their partner leaves.

▲ **Science Area**—A special science area, created as a permanent part of the classroom, allows children repeated opportunities to engage in the scientific process as they examine displays and experiment with simple machines and a variety of materials. Children can return again and again to repeat the process and see if the results are the same. They can also alter certain aspects of their experimentation and watch for changes in the outcome. For example, children might raise the height of a ramp and observe how this affects the speed of cars rolling down it.

Opportunities for children to better understand science and its relationship to their world arise repeatedly in a whole-science classroom. From wiping up accidental juice spills with an absorbent napkin, to watching paint dripping from a picture on an easel, the ramifications of science are everywhere. Teachers can capitalize on these many possibilities to create science-rich classrooms.

The Whole-Science Child
What are some characteristics of children accustomed to whole-science classrooms?

Children in constructivist classrooms, especially those rich in potential for scientific learning, do not wait for teachers to tell them how to find information or solve problems. Instead, they react as a scientist might, envisioning possibilities, experimenting with how objects react, and observing the results.

Children are natural scientists. They poke and prod whatever they discover. This is how children obtain the raw data necessary to form relationships—to learn. Children in whole-science classrooms retain this experimental fervor. They do not hang back and wait for the teacher to tell them the one correct way to use a tool or a list of attributes to memorize about a material. Rather, they expect to discover things for themselves as they explore. Children are the problem solvers. Children are the scientists.

What is the developmental stage of preschool and kindergarten children?

Preschool and kindergarten children are in a stage of cognitive development that Piaget calls preoperational.[1] Although preoperational children experience extensive language growth that helps them solve cognitive problems, their perceptions still sway their logical thinking. This leads children to magical thinking in science. Young children may initially think that it is magical that glue holds seeds on paper. Repeated experiences lead them to the understanding that adhesion is a physical property of glue.

Young children are egocentric. They tend to view scientific phenomena personally. Thus one child thinks it's his birthday because he notices it is snowing outside. Another child believes that dried corn kernels turns to powder because of her magic. It might take several experiences before she can relate the corn's change in form to her pounding the corn with a mortar and pestle. Preoperational children believe that the moon is following them and their thoughts can make things happen.

What are the types of knowledge that children construct?

Piaget describes three types of knowledge: socially transmitted, physical, and logical-mathematical.[2]

- ▲ *Socially transmitted knowledge* is arbitrary, such as the names of objects or social customs. It is the one type of knowledge that has to be told to children, either directly or through books.
- ▲ *Physical knowledge* involves the physical properties of materials, such as weight, shape, roughness, or fluidity. Children construct physical knowledge through examination and by physically acting on objects and observing the results. They need many opportunities for experimentation with physical materials in order to understand the underlying scientific concepts. The bulk of the science curriculum should involve physical-knowledge activities.
- ▲ *Logical-mathematical knowledge* involves the formation of relationships, such as more or less, heavier or lighter, or partially floating. Measurement and quantification are also logical-mathematical relationships. Logical-mathematical knowledge must be constructed internally by each individual. Physical knowledge explorations provide the information from which many logical-mathematical relationships are constructed. Thus, the two types of knowledge often develop together.

How do the three types of knowledge relate to science education?

Most scientific knowledge, particularly with young children, falls into the physical knowledge area. This should be reflected in both the curriculum and the teacher's approach. When teachers try to socially transmit physical knowledge, such as telling children that heavy objects sink, or reading aloud to children about simple machines, children do not understand. Instead, they may develop a surface knowledge that allows them to parrot information back without fully understanding the concepts. Thus, they cannot use the information to solve problems or create new relationships.

The following are some specific examples of how Piaget's three types of knowledge affect science education with young children.

- ▲ *Socially Transmitted Knowledge*—The direct teaching of scientific information should primarily be limited to providing correct labels, as for shells or animals, and the scientific terms for processes, such as *absorption*. Socially transmitted knowledge should never be the primary focus of a science activity.

- ▲ *Physical Knowledge*—Most science activities in this book involve physical knowledge as children act on objects and observe the results. Scraping, rolling, swinging, pounding, prying, twisting, and squeezing are some of the actions children engage in that encourage the construction of physical knowledge.

- ▲ *Logical-Mathematical Knowledge*—Logical-mathematical knowledge is intertwined with physical knowledge in most science activities. As children make comparisons, such as which material absorbs the most water, or notice cause and effect relationships, such as how raising a pendulum affects its ability to knock down blocks, they are constructing logical-mathematical knowledge.

Is whole-science appropriate for all children?

Yes! All children learn by physically interacting with materials and observing the results. This is often particularly evident in children with cognitive disabilities. They may spend even more time repeating physical explorations of materials than typically developing children.

Do children ever come to incorrect conclusions?

Of course, and so do scientists. As children continue to develop and mature, and as they have more and more experiences with materials, they revise their hypotheses and alter their conclusions. This is the same way scientific theories change and knowledge advances in the realm of science.

The Whole-Science Teacher

What are the characteristics of an effective whole-science teacher?

An effective whole-science teacher develops a curriculum that encourages scientific exploration in all areas of the classroom throughout the day. The skillful whole-science teacher:

▲ Creates a classroom atmosphere that encourages children to experiment and solve problems

▲ Guides children in following the scientific process

▲ Facilitates the construction of knowledge through carefully formulated comments and questions that encourage thinking

▲ Takes advantage of opportunities for exploring science whenever they arise

▲ Plans activities that build on one another and correlate with the rest of the curriculum

▲ Helps children communicate about science and record their observations

How can teachers encourage children to think scientifically?

Teachers can encourage children to follow the scientific process, just as a scientist would. They can structure their activities and questions to help children:

▲ Hypothesize and Predict

▲ Experiment

▲ Observe

▲ Compare and Classify

▲ Infer

▲ Measure

▲ Communicate

▲ Create Relationships

What should teachers do when children come to incorrect conclusions?

Teachers can plan additional activities that focus on the same concept. They can also use questions and comments to direct chil-

dren's attention to certain relationships or outcomes. For example, children often draw incorrect conclusions as they explore the relationship between the size of an instrument and its pitch, or how high or low it sounds. They may mislabel a large drum as high and a small drum as low because the large drum looks physically higher off the ground. Teachers can plan many additional activities that enable children to explore size and pitch relationships with a variety of instruments. They can also continue to model correct pitch labels as they sing or play instruments.

Teachers can also use questions or comments to focus children's observations. For example, it typically takes children a long time to understand where to place bottles in order for a pendulum to knock them down. Some children decide the pendulum is broken because its arc carries it over their bottles. Teachers can encourage children without correcting them, as with the following comment and questions:

"I noticed that the pendulum always flies over the bottles."
"Is there a place where the pendulum is closer to the ground?"
"What do you think would happen if you put the bottles there?"

Why do whole-science teachers avoid correcting errors?

Whole-science teachers recognize that errors are a reflection of the child's current level of thinking and are developmentally appropriate. Correcting children's errors may inhibit their explorations and cause them to look to adults for answers rather than seeking solutions themselves.

Instead of directly correcting misconceptions, teachers can focus on curriculum that encourages logical rather than magical thinking. This is why physical knowledge activities are so valuable, while experiments that do not involve direct manipulation by children are not. Releasing a ball and cube down a ramp involves some direct participation of children in controlling the outcome. Watching colored water creep up a celery stalk does not. Activities such as the latter are more likely to reinforce magical thinking.

Why don't whole-science teachers rely on books or teacher-directed experiments to teach science?

Books and teacher-directed experiments involve the social transmission of knowledge and do not encourage the scientific process. Children need direct experience with materials and control over determining the direction of their explorations in order to construct scientific knowledge. Books can be used to augment this knowledge or to look up terminology but cannot substitute for direct experience.

How can teachers assess children's development of scientific knowledge?

Teachers can carefully observe children as they interact with materials and ask pertinent questions to delve into their thinking. They can take anecdotal notes as children explore scientific principles throughout the curriculum. Teachers can also record information on assessment forms, such as those included in the appendix. "Terms and Definitions" can be found in appendix A.2. Blank forms for individual and class assessment are located in appendices A.3 and A.4.

How can teachers develop and display materials that encourage the construction of scientific knowledge?

Teachers can create a science area in their classrooms. They can assemble natural objects, commercial science materials, or teacher-constructed items to display in the area. Teachers can develop many science activities that involve typical classroom materials used in unique ways. They can build scientific apparatuses using inexpensive materials. The activities in this book give suggestions and specific directions.

How can this book help teachers develop a science-rich classroom?

The following chapters describe ways in which teachers can encourage the exploration of scientific principles in many areas of the classroom. While science is embedded in many of the ongoing activities in an early childhood classroom, it can also be encouraged through carefully designed activities. As teachers and children explore science through the activities in this book, new curriculum ideas will likely emerge. Teachers are encouraged to follow children's inclinations and their own creative ideas as they develop new avenues for scientific discovery in their classrooms.

ENDNOTES

1. Barry J. Wadsworth, *Piaget's Theory of Cognitive and Affective Development*, 4th ed. (White Plains, NY: Longman, 1989) 59 ff.
2. Wadsworth, 21–24.

Science Displays

Claire sat at the science table spinning the tops displayed on a tray. She was delighted when one of them made spiral marks on the paper. Michael and Bobby ran over and stood next to the table. Michael reached out to stop the top and Bobby said, "Again!" The two boys did not have the fine-motor dexterity to make the tops spin. They stayed nearby for ten minutes and watched Claire continue to spin the tops. She made each top spin as they made a gesture or used a single word to ask for more.

▲ ▲ ▲

Shi-cheng carefully examined each gourd by touching, smelling, and shaking. He gasped as he shook a dried one, which sounded like a rattle. He called for the teacher to come over. As she arrived he pointed excitedly to the dried gourd. He handed one to her and gestured a shaking motion. The two of them continued the exploration at Shi-cheng's direction. Finally he separated the gourds into groups. One group included all the fresh gourds and the other included all the dried gourds.

▲ ▲ ▲

Imagine yourself as a young child on a visit to a museum. You probably can't see into most of the cases, and you can't read the information signs. Your parents may have to read the descriptions, which detail the life cycle of a butterfly or the habitat of a snake. Now imagine you are a child in a contemporary children's museum that encourages interaction with the materials. The displays are low and open and invite you to touch the objects. The information signs contain questions your parents can ask you to make you think about what you are doing or to introduce new vocabulary as you interact with the materials. You dig for fossils in a sandpit or you try to hold back a stream of water by building a dam of wooden blocks.

Similar displays of science materials are a part of science-rich early childhood classrooms. Children are naturally drawn to attractive displays of materials, such as pinecones, or more unusual objects, such as tops. The materials provide opportunities for children to:

▲ Hypothesize

▲ Observe

▲ Predict

▲ Compare and Classify

▲ Infer

▲ Measure

▲ Communicate

▲ Create Relationships

This is science! The biologist, paleontologist, medical researcher, and meteorologist participate in the processes listed above.

Teachers' Questions
What is a science display?

A science display is a group of related objects for children to handle and explore. They may pick up the objects, look at them, touch them, smell them, shake them, or move them using a tool, such as tongs or tweezers. As they interact with the materials, they develop a better understanding of the physical properties of each object; they begin to create relationships among the objects.

Why is it important to include science displays in the curriculum?

Science displays encourage children to handle materials they might otherwise avoid. As children explore the materials, they participate in the scientific process. They gain confidence in their own abilities, expand their vocabularies, hypothesize or create problems to solve, observe similarities and differences, make comparisons, classify materials based on common attributes, measure, make cause and effect inferences, and communicate with one another. Young children have often been told *not* to touch beautiful objects or even natural materials in the environment. Science displays provide a safe setting for children to explore inviting materials.

What makes a good science display?

A good display includes natural materials or other intriguing objects for children to observe, but more importantly to handle, in order to more closely observe similarities and differences. Science displays may also encourage children to hypothesize, compare, classify, measure, infer, and communicate with one another. Displays may be part of a thematic unit and therefore provide opportunities for children to create relationships to materials in other curricular areas. For example, the teacher might display a selection of corn that includes a variety of colors and two different sizes of ears of corn (activity 2.5). The illustrations on the wall behind the area could include autumn scenes, such as pumpkins, gourds, and colorful foliage, as well as corn.

What is wrong with the displays described in many activity books?

Activity books often suggest displays of objects that can be grouped by predetermined categories, such as big and small or tall and short. These types of activities do not encourage children to consider other possibilities. Children believe that the teacher already knows the answer. There is no reason for them to think, hypothesize, or try solutions to problems they may design. Activity books or curriculum guides often suggest using a magnifying glass for closer observation of the objects. While children enjoy using the magnifying glass to look at the objects, the activity books may not provide adequate information for teachers to ensure that the children fully participate in the scientific process.

Science activity books generally do not address the issue of the integrated curriculum. If a display is not an integrated part of the curriculum, children may not be able to create as many relationships among the classroom materials. Educators know that repeated experiences with the same or related materials lead to higher attention to detail and new learning. The activities in this book give teachers suggestions for integrated curriculum activities.

What scientific processes emerge as children interact with materials in the science displays?

As children interact with science display materials, they hypothesize, create problems to solve, observe, compare, classify, measure, infer, and communicate, both orally and in writing. The displays are accessible to all children at a wide range of developmental levels. For example, one child may request the verbal label for pinecone, while another child may group the pinecones by attributes, such as size or type. A third child may order the pinecones by size, from the smallest to the largest. In each of these examples, the children either communicate, classify, or measure—all of which are components of the scientific process.

What are the easiest displays for teachers to assemble?

Natural materials from the local environment are the easiest displays to assemble. They are readily available, free or inexpensive, and a part of the children's experiences. They can be quickly assembled from parks or backyards and are interesting to young children. For example, the display might include a collection of walnuts, acorns, and buckeye nuts, several clear jars, and a pair of tongs (activity 2.2). The children can observe, make comparisons, and classify the nuts by placing them into the clear jars, using the tongs as a tool.

What kinds of displays should the teacher consider?

Teachers may plan a display specific to the particular season or coordinate the display with a thematic topic as part of the integrated curriculum. The teacher may also choose a particular display to stimulate more interest in the science area. For example, a display of small tops is very different and may attract children who otherwise avoid the science area. A collection of gourds, some dried and some fresh, is also unusual. Children may be drawn to the area to shake the dried gourds and compare them to the more vividly colored fresh gourds.

Where can the science displays be placed in the classroom?

A science area can be designed to encourage children to explore the displays. Teachers may define the area with a table, a low bench or shelf, or a more nontraditional display surface, such as a tree stump or a large rock. The table or bench can be covered with a piece of carpet or felt to provide added interest. The tree stump or flat rock will be naturally intriguing to children. Science displays are enhanced by the addition of related illustrations. Place the display surface against a wall, a pegboard room divider, or the back of a shelf to provide a place to mount the pictures.

How long should the displays be in the science area?

The displays are typically left in the area for two to three weeks, or longer if needed. Science displays, like many other curricular materials, require an extended period of exploration. Since many of the displays coordinate with other areas of the classroom, they will follow the same schedule as the thematic topic. In many cases the displays change slightly each week in order to further the thinking of the children, pose new possibilities, or sustain interest.

Where can teachers find the supplies for the science displays?

Teachers can find all of the supplies for the seasonal displays in the neighborhood surrounding the school, parks, grocery and produce stores, and in some cases, the children's backyard. Parents are usually a good resource as well. Teachers usually are inundated with nature items once the word gets out that they are collecting. Many families seem to have a supply of shells, acorns, and rocks. Craft supply stores also carry a variety of natural materials, including some unique specimens.

How do teachers initially set up the display?

The general rule is to start slowly with a smaller number of items in the display so children can fully explore them without feeling overwhelmed. When children are readily able to view all the materials and easily handle them, they are less likely to misuse them. This chapter's activity section provides specific information for each display. The sequence of information details types and quantities of items to display. The "Helpful Hints" in each activity provides information to help teachers avoid some of the potential problems as well.

What is the teacher's role?

The teacher sets up the science display, makes encouraging statements as children interact with the materials, and asks well-timed, developmentally appropriate questions. Teachers usually want to impart information because that seems like a teacher's job. In the area of science, teachers must avoid this thinking so that children can come up with interesting problems of their own to solve. We want children to be confident in their own abilities and think of themselves as scientists.

How can teachers assess the development of children's scientific knowledge?

Teachers can choose to keep a notebook of anecdotal records or use an observation-based assessment sheet. A sample of an observation tool for science displays is included in appendix A.5.

Activities with Displays

2.1 Food for Winter
Acorns

Description
A collection of interesting acorns encourages children to think about similarities and differences as they observe and handle the nuts. The display is especially appropriate in early autumn when acorns are plentiful and some animals gather them to store for winter.

Child's Level
This display is appropriate for preschool and kindergarten children.

Materials
- ▲ 25–30 acorns in a variety of sizes and types, with and without caps
- ▲ several clear plastic jars or tumblers for sorting the nuts
- ▲ a basket for displaying the nuts
- ▲ illustrations of acorns, oak trees, and squirrels
- ▲ tongs (optional)

Scientific Information
Acorns—the fruit of oak trees—have caps on top of the nut; the nut and cap vary by type of oak tree. Some nuts are edible by humans and some are edible only by animals. Some animals store acorns as a winter food source.

Sequence of Implementation
1. Begin with 15–20 acorns that vary by size and type.
2. Add one or more variations, such as acorns without the cap or green acorns.
3. Add the tongs and clear jars or tumblers for sorting the acorns.

What to Look For
Children will handle the acorns and notice similarities and differences.

Some children will group the acorns according to size or type of acorn.

Some children will communicate personal experiences about squirrels and acorns.

Questions to Extend Thinking
Which of these acorns go together? (Ask this if the child is
     handling the acorns but not observing the similarities or
     differences.)
Are there any other acorns like these?
How do you think squirrels crack open the acorns?

Modifications
Add word cards to the display. Mount illustrations of an acorn,
     oak leaf, and squirrel onto separate index cards. Label the pic-
     tures and cover the cards with laminate film or contact paper.
Reduce or add to the quantities of acorns based on the needs of
     the group.

Integrated Curriculum Activities
Glue acorns onto cardboard as an art activity.
Take a nature walk to gather local varieties of acorns.
Place acorns, tongs, and ice cube trays in the sensory table (activ-
     ity 4.12).
Use acorn caps as counters for a math game. See *More Than
     Counting: Whole Math Activities for Preschool and Kindergarten*,
     by Sally Moomaw and Brenda Hieronymus, activity 4.5.

Helpful Hint
Use a glue gun to secure some of the caps to the acorns.

2.2 Nuts to You
Nuts and Peanuts

Description
A collection of interesting nuts encourages children to closely observe similarities and differences and to classify by common attributes. The addition of peanuts, familiar to children, draws them to the collection. This display is especially appropriate in late autumn when the nuts are plentiful in grocery stores.

Child's Level
This display is appropriate for preschool and kindergarten children.

Materials
▲ variety of nuts, such as walnuts, pecans, Brazil nuts, and almonds
▲ selection of peanuts
▲ nutcracker
▲ basket for displaying the collection
▲ divided tray for sorting the nuts
▲ illustrations of nuts in the display

Scientific Information
A nut is the fruit of some trees. Peanuts are related to pea and bean plants, which contain seeds inside a pod. The peanut is not a nut; it is a pod with beans inside. These beans, like the nuts from trees, are the seeds of the plant. Some nuts and peanuts are edible by humans. The edible portion of the nut is inside a hard outer shell. Shells with cracks in them are easier to open. Nuts and peanuts vary in color, shape, size, texture, taste, and ease of opening.

Sequence of Implementation
1. Begin with 8–10 nuts in each of three varieties. Do not include peanuts in the initial display.
2. Add 8–10 nuts in one or two more types.
3. Add a nutcracker and peanuts.

What to Look For
Some children may closely observe the nuts, especially the less
   common varieties.
Many children will not know the names of the nuts.
Some children will attempt to open each type of nut.
Children will be very excited to use the nutcracker to open nuts.

Questions to Extend Thinking
Which of these do you think will be the hardest to open? The
   easiest?
Are there any other nuts with a crack in the shell? Will they be
   easier to open?
I found one with a circle design. Are there any more like this one?

Modifications
Add a tree identification book to the display. These books usually
   include an illustration of the tree, the leaf, and the fruit (nut).
Add word cards to the display. Glue an illustration of each nut
   onto a separate index card. Label the card and cover with laminate film or contact paper.

Integrated Curriculum Activities
Make almond butter as a cooking activity.
Open some of the nuts at group time and make comparisons or
   perform taste tests.
Have children estimate the number of nuts in a clear plastic jar.
Read books about animals that eat nuts and peanuts, such as
   Squirrels, by Brian Wildsmith, and *Nuts to You!,* by Lois Ehlert.

Helpful Hint
A collection of nuts used solely as a display can be kept for
several years.

2.3 Seeds and Seed Carriers
Seeds in Autumn

Description
This autumn display includes a variety of seeds and seed pods from the local environment. The display is especially valuable in autumn when many plants produce seeds.

Child's Level
This display is appropriate for preschool and kindergarten children.

Materials
- ▲ a variety of plant seeds, such as sunflower, pumpkin, carrot, bean
- ▲ seed carriers, such as thistle, milkweed pods, locust pods, and maple seeds (whirlybirds)

Scientific Information
Certain trees grow from seeds. Some of the seeds are enclosed in a papery wing and carried by the wind. Some tree seeds are enclosed inside a fleshy fruit that animals eat. The animal doesn't digest the seed; it passes out in the droppings and germinates in the spring. Other seeds are inside nuts that animals eat. The seeds that are eaten are digested. Animals who store food for winter, however, sometimes forget where they hid the nuts and these germinate in the spring.

Sequence of Implementation
1. Start with locust and lily pods and the sunflower and bean seeds.
2. Introduce additional seeds that vary in attributes, such as maple seeds (whirlybird), pumpkin seeds (large), and carrot seeds (small).
3. Add additional types of seed pods, such as milkweed.

What to Look For
Some children will closely examine the seeds and pods.
Some children will shake the pods and break them open.

Questions to Extend Thinking

Are there any seeds that are the same size? Same color? Same
   type?
What plant do you think grows from this seed?
How could an animal help move this seed?
How would this seed move by the wind?

Modification

Add magnifying glasses to encourage close observation.

Integrated Curriculum Activities

Glue seeds onto cardboard as an art activity.
Place seeds, small plastic jars, and spoons in the sensory table.
Allow children to try to move some seeds, such as maple seeds,
   by using a fan or bellows.
Take a nature walk and collect seeds and pods.
Use large seed pods, such as locust pods, for maracas
   (activity 6.10).

Helpful Hint

Store the seeds and seed pods in open containers to avoid the formation of mold.

2.4 Ornamental Gourds
Varieties of Gourds

Description
This autumn display of ornamental gourds includes a selection of fresh and dried gourds in different types, sizes, and colors.

Child's Level
This display is appropriate for preschool and kindergarten children.

Materials
- ▲ selection of fresh ornamental gourds
- ▲ selection of dried ornamental gourds
- ▲ basket for displaying the gourds
- ▲ sign that reads *Some gourds are fresh. Some gourds have dried.*
- ▲ illustrations of autumn scenes, pumpkins, gourds, corn stalks, etc.

Scientific Information
Ornamental gourds change in color and weight over time. The seeds inside the dried gourds may create a sound when the gourds are shaken. Some gourds rot as they age, while others dry out.

Sequence of Implementation
1. Begin with a selection of fresh gourds that vary by size, color, and type.
2. After one week of exploration, add a selection of dried gourds that are similar to the fresh ones.
3. After one week add the sign *Some gourds are fresh. Some gourds have dried.*

What to Look For
Children will handle the gourds to explore the physical properties. Some children will attempt to open the gourds. Many children will shake the dried gourds.

Questions to Extend Thinking
Can you find a dried gourd like this fresh one?
Do all of the gourds make a sound?
What is happening to this one? (Point to one beginning to dry.)

Modification
Add pencil and paper for children to record predictions about the contents of the gourds. Open some of the gourds to verify the predictions.

Integrated Curriculum Activities
Include teacher-made shakers in the music area (activity 6.10).
Open some of the gourds as a special activity. Plant some of the seeds.
Scrub gourds in the sensory table.
Use a balance to compare the weights of fresh and dried gourds (activity 3.9).

Helpful Hint
Place gourds in a cool space to dry for use the next year. Check periodically to remove ones that begin to rot.

2.5 Corn-ucopia
Varieties of Corn

Description
This display may include one or more varieties of ears of corn, such as feed corn, ornamental corn, and popcorn. Children may compare the physical properties—texture, color, and size—of the varieties of corn.

Child's Level
This display is appropriate for preschool and kindergarten children.

Materials
▲ selection of feed corn and other varieties of corn, such as yellow, white, purple, multicolored, and popcorn on the cob
▲ illustrations of autumn scenes, such as trees or corn fields
▲ cornstalk, if possible

Scientific Information
Animals eat feed corn. People eat many varieties of corn. The indigenous people of North and South America originally cultivated corn. The kernels of different types of corn vary in color, size, and shape.

Sequence of Implementation
1. Display several different colors of corn, feed corn, and popcorn on the cob.
2. Add black popcorn and miniature varieties of corncobs.
3. Add a cornstalk.

What to Look For
Some children are unfamiliar with the materials and may need to know the labels for the items.
Children will examine the corn and make comparisons.
Some children will remove the kernels from the cobs.

Questions to Extend Thinking
Does this corn look like the corn that you eat?
How are these two ears of corn the same? How are they different?

Modification
Add tweezers to the display to provide opportunities to remove the kernels from the cob using a simple machine (activity 3.10).

Integrated Curriculum Activities
Put kernels of corn into the sensory table with funnels and
    buckets.
Glue kernels of colored corn onto cardboard as an art activity.
Plan to pop several varieties of popcorn.
Place feed corn in a nearby tree to feed the birds and squirrels.
Grind corn to make cornmeal (activities 3.11 and 3.12).
Sing songs about animals collecting corn. See *More Than Singing:*
    Discovering Music in Preschool and Kindergarten, by Sally
    Moomaw, activity 6.10.
Read *The Popcorn Book,* by Tomie de Paola.

Helpful Hint
Purchase feed corn at a local feed store.

2.6 Pumpkin Parade
Varieties of Pumpkins

Description
Children may already be familiar with pumpkins. This display includes a variety of types of pumpkins so children may compare them through observation and handling.

Child's Level
This display is appropriate for preschool and kindergarten children.

Materials
- ▲ several mature orange pumpkins in different sizes
- ▲ unusual varieties of pumpkins, such as a white pumpkin
- ▲ illustrations of pumpkins, fields of pumpkins, scarecrows, etc.

Scientific Information
Pumpkins grow on vines and come in different colors, shapes, and sizes. They all have a series of lines or indentations that travel from the stem to the bottom of the pumpkin. Pumpkins have many seeds inside the shell.

Sequence of Implementation
1. Display the familiar orange pumpkins first.
2. Add the more unusual pumpkins after one week of display.

What to Look For
Some children will attempt to lift the pumpkins.
Some children will compare the pumpkins.
Some children will count the lines on the pumpkins.
Many children will communicate their personal experiences with pumpkins.

Questions to Extend Thinking
Where do these pumpkins grow?
Do all of these pumpkins have the same number of lines?
What do you think is inside the pumpkin?

Modification

Add paper and pencils for children to record their observations and predictions.

Integrated Curriculum Activities

Scrub pumpkins in the sensory table.

For comparison, open an ornamental gourd shaped like a miniature pumpkin, a pie pumpkin, and the traditional carving pumpkin.

Toast pumpkin seeds as a cooking activity.

Glue pumpkin seeds onto paper as an art activity.

Visit a farm to see how pumpkins grow.

Graph predictions of where pumpkins grow. See *More Than Counting,* by Sally Moomaw and Brenda Hieronymus, activity 6.6.

Children can write or dictate stories in pumpkin-shaped books.

Include the book *Pumpkin Pumpkin,* by Jeanne Titherington, in the reading area. It describes a little boy's experiences observing the life cycle of a pumpkin.

Helpful Hint

Local farmers often grow unusual varieties of pumpkins.

2.7 Pinecone Potpourri
Varieties of Pinecones

Description
Children can compare the physical properties of pinecones in this display. They may or may not be aware that the pine nuts inside some pinecones are edible. The display is appropriate in winter or spring or can be repeated twice during the year.

Child's Level
This display is appropriate for preschool and kindergarten children.

Materials
▲ collection of pinecones in a variety of sizes and types
▲ illustrations of pine trees, pinecones, and animals eating the seeds

Scientific Information
Pinecones open when they are ready to drop the seeds. Pinecones differ in size, color, and shape. Some pine nuts are edible by both humans and animals.

Sequence of Implementation
1. Begin with five or six pinecones of one type, which vary in size.
2. Change the selection after one week of exploration to include several different types and sizes of pinecones.
3. Add some unusual sizes of pinecones, such as Ponderosa Pine (very large) and pinecones from potpourri (very small).

What to Look For
Children may sequence the pinecones from smallest to largest.
Children may observe the similarities and differences as they compare the pinecones.
Children may communicate their observations of the pinecones.

Questions to Extend Thinking
What do you notice about these two pinecones?
Is there another pinecone that is like this one?
Why do you think this pinecone is closed?

Modification

Display some pinecones that have been stored overnight in a bucket of cold water so they close tightly.

Integrated Curriculum Activities

Use pinecones with glitter and glue as an art activity.

Paint the pinecones as an art activity.

Make a bird feeder with peanut butter and bird seed. Make sure to provide a sufficient water source for the birds that use the feeder.

Read *The Big Tree and The Little Tree,* by Mary Augusta Lappage. It describes the environmental value of pine trees from a Native American perspective.

Take a field trip to observe pinecones on trees or collect pinecones from the ground.

Helpful Hint

Look for large pinecones in craft stores.

2.8 Nature's Nursery
Bird Nests

Description
This display allows children to closely observe bird nests that are typically out of their reach. They can easily compare the materials used in different nests. Displays of bird nests can be implemented in early winter, when the nests are visible in the bare trees, and again in spring, when birds build nests.

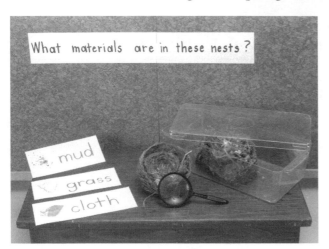

What materials are in these nests?

mud
grass
cloth

Child's Level
This display is most appropriate for older preschool and kindergarten children. Younger children may be more interested in pulling apart the nests.

Materials
▲ several bird nests (you may need to replace them each week)
▲ plastic boxes with clear lids
▲ illustrations of birds and bird nests
▲ magnifying glasses

Scientific Information
Birds combine such materials as dirt, string, and grass to form unique structures.

Sequence of Implementation
1. Consider beginning with a display of nests enclosed in sealed plastic boxes with clear lids.
2. Include magnifying glasses for closer observation.
3. Add similar nests in other varieties for children to handle.

What to Look For
Children will be very curious about the contents of the nests and may want to pull apart some of the materials.

Some children will communicate with each other about their observations.

Some children will handle the nests very carefully as they explore them.

Questions to Extend Thinking

What materials are in these nests?

Where do you think the bird found this string (or other component)?

Modifications

Make word cards to add to the display. Glue samples of the components birds use to build nests, such as dirt and string, onto separate index cards. Label each card with the name of the material and cover with laminate film or contact paper. Include the sign *What materials are in these nests?*

Provide paper and pencils for children to record their observations of the materials in the nests.

Integrated Curriculum Activities

Include the books *Bird Nests,* by Eileen Curran, and *Feathers for Lunch,* by Lois Ehlert, in the reading area.

Paint with feathers as an art activity.

Older children may be able to use dirt, string, grass, etc., to create a nest.

Use small bird nests and plastic eggs from a craft store for a math game. See *More Than Counting,* by Sally Moomaw and Brenda Hieronymus, activity 2.2.

Sing songs about birds. See *More Than Singing,* by Sally Moomaw, activity 2.2.

Play recordings of bird songs.

Helpful Hint

Nests will be more visible for collection during late autumn, when the trees are more bare.

2.9 A Spring Tradition
Varieties of Seeds

Description
This display will help children focus on seeds that are planted in the spring and produce a flower or vegetable plant. They will be able to compare seeds and compare seeds to the final plants.

Child's Level
This display is appropriate for older preschool and kindergarten children.

Materials
▲ a variety of seeds from tomatoes, pumpkins, bean, sunflowers, avocados, marigolds, etc.
▲ tweezers
▲ magnifying glasses
▲ divided tray for displaying the seeds
▲ illustrations of plants and seeds

Scientific Information
Some plants grow from seeds. Children often expect that the size, shape, and color of a seed are related to the size, shape, and color of the plant that grows from it. Experience with sprouting seeds helps children understand that this is usually not the case.

Sequence of Implementation
1. Display the largest seeds first (sunflower, pumpkin, bean).
2. Add one or two different varieties of seeds and tweezers for picking up the seeds.
3. Add tomato seeds (very tiny) and avocado seeds (very large).
4. Add magnifying glasses.

What to Look For

Some children may initially pour the seeds in and out of the display container.

Some children may group seeds by type.

Children may compare seeds to one another.

Many children will communicate their observations of the seeds.

Some children may infer which type of plant will grow from which seed. They may expect large plants to grow from big seeds.

Questions to Extend Thinking

What plant do you think will grow from this seed?

Do any of these seeds go together?

Modification

Add the packets for the displayed seeds and provide paper and pencils for children to copy the names of the plants.

Integrated Curriculum Activities

Glue some of the seeds onto paper as an art activity.

Plant several varieties of the displayed seeds. Group seeds by type for ease of comparison after the plants have grown.

Include the book *This Year's Garden,* by Cynthia Rylant, in the reading area.

Use empty seed packets at the writing center so that children can copy the names of flowers and vegetables.

Estimate how many seeds are in some of the fruits or vegetables served at lunch.

Helpful Hint

Outdated seeds for display purposes only may be available either free or inexpensively from a local nursery.

2.10 Tropical Wonders
Coconuts

Description
This display of coconuts includes as many types as are available. The display encourages children to explore the properties of items to which they may not typically have access.

Child's Level
This display is appropriate for preschool and kindergarten children.

Materials
▲ several coconut seeds
▲ coconut in the outer shell
▲ coconut seed cut into halves
▲ sign that reads *What is inside the coconut?*
▲ slips of paper and pencils

Scientific Information
Coconuts have a thick oval husk that is brown and fibrous. They are the fruit of the coconut palm. The hairy "coconut" found in grocery stores is actually just the seed of the coconut. Within the thin, hard shell of a coconut seed is layer of edible white meat. The center is filled with a cloudy substance called coconut milk.

Sequence of Implementation
1. Begin with a display of the inside seed of the coconut. This is the type found in the grocery store. If available, include a coconut in the outer shell.
2. Add the sign *What is inside the coconut?* Put out pencils and slips of paper for children to record their predictions. Cut open a coconut to verify the predictions.
3. Add some coconut shells cut into halves.

What to Look For
Children may pick up the coconuts to touch the "hairy" outside.
Children may shake the coconut to hear the liquid.
Children may compare the attributes of the outside and inside of the coconut.

Questions to Extend Thinking
How is this coconut different from this one?
What happens when you shake this one?
What do you think is inside this coconut?

Modification
Shred some of the coconut meat and add to the display.

Integrated Curriculum Activities
Use dried halves of coconut shells as musical instruments.
Open a coconut and taste the insides.
Compare the taste of fresh coconut milk and fresh coconut pulp
    to processed milk and dried, shredded coconut pulp.
Include the books *Coconut Kind of Day,* by Lynn Joseph, and
    Chicka Chicka Boom Boom, by Bill Martin Jr. and John
    Archambault, in the reading area.

Helpful Hint
It takes a long time to slice a coconut in half. Use a saw.

2.11 Earth Treasures
Rocks and Minerals

Description
Common indigenous rocks, as well as some unfamiliar rocks and minerals, comprise this beautiful display. Children will eagerly handle the rocks and minerals to explore their attributes. They may compare the weight, color, texture, and shape of the rocks and minerals.

Child's Level
This display is appropriate for older preschool and kindergarten children.

Materials
- ▲ rocks gathered from the local environment
- ▲ minerals gathered or purchased at museums or other shops
- ▲ cup of water
- ▲ penny or other metal disk
- ▲ magnifying glasses

Scientific Information
Rocks are made of minerals. Some are made of only one mineral; most are made of more than one kind of mineral. Minerals vary in weight, color, texture, and type. Some minerals are soft and some are very hard. The hardness of minerals helps us identify them. Colored rocks and minerals can be crushed and the powder used to make paints.

Sequence of Implementation
1. Display four or five rocks and minerals during the initial week. Select different colors and sizes.
2. Change a few of the rocks and minerals during subsequent weeks of the display.
3. Add a small cup of water. Children can dip the rocks and minerals into the water and observe the changes in appearance.
4. Add the penny or metal disk. Children can scratch the surface and check the degree of hardness of the rocks and minerals.

What to Look For
Children may want to test their strength by lifting the rocks and
    minerals.
Children may compare the size, weight, color, and type of rocks
    and minerals.
Children may communicate their observations.

Questions to Extend Thinking
How are these two rocks the same? How are they different?
What happens when you dip this rock into the water?

Modifications
Add a rock and mineral identification book to the display.
Use hammers to crack open geodes. If geodes are not indigenous
    to your area, you can purchase them at science and nature
    stores. Be sure children wear safety glasses.

Integrated Curriculum Activities
Paint rocks as an art activity.
Take a walk in search of rocks.
Visit a local store that sells rocks and minerals.
Call a local university geology department. Ask for a guest
    speaker to visit or for a tour of their facilities.

Helpful Hint
Ask parents for donations of rocks and minerals. Try to acquire a
large piece of mica. It is formed in many layers that children can
peel for years before it is used up.

2.12 Ancient Treasures
Fossils

Description
This display is one that is best implemented in an area where fossils are a natural part of the local environment. This enables you and the children to make connections to familiar objects.

Child's Level
This display is appropriate for older preschool and kindergarten children.

Materials
- ▲ fossils gathered from the local environment or purchased at museum and nature stores
- ▲ illustrations of fossils and the plants and animals that formed the fossils
- ▲ magnifying glasses

Scientific Information
Fossils were formed long ago from the remains of plants and animals. A fossil may result from plant or animal material that has been replaced by minerals. Fossils may also be stone molds or casts created when the hard parts of organisms were dissolved by groundwater. Scientists gain knowledge of the distant past from the fossils of plants and animals.

Sequence of Implementation
1. Begin with fossils that are similar to familiar plants and animals in the environment today, such as ocean shells and snail shells.
2. Add more unfamiliar types of fossils.
3. Introduce a slab of rock with embedded fossils.
4. For comparison, introduce seashells that are similar to some of the fossils.

What to Look For
Some children may compare the fossils to the pictures of the fossils.

Some children may communicate personal information about fossils.

Some children may relate fossils to familiar objects, such as seashells.

Questions to Extend Thinking
Can you find any fossils that look like this picture?

Are there any other fossils like this one?

What type of animal do you think this was?

Modification
Add a fossil identification book to the display.

Integrated Curriculum Activities
Press fossils into playdough or other dough to make impressions (activity 5.22).

Bury fossils in a pan of sand and use small instruments to dig for them.

Include the book *Digging Up Dinosaurs,* by Aliki.

Scrub fossils in the sensory table (activity 4.18).

Call a local university geology department. Ask for a guest speaker to visit or for a tour of their facilities.

Helpful Hint
Local clubs or amateur collectors may be willing to donate fossils to your school.

2.13 Sea Treasures
Shells

Description
This display is appealing because of the nature of the shape, texture, and colors of shells. The cold, hard shells seem to invite us to handle them. The physical features of shells are very different from natural items found away from the ocean. Even children who have daily access to sand, water, and shells seem to find enjoyment in the explorations of a display such as this.

Child's Level
This display is appropriate for preschool and kindergarten children. Even the youngest preschool child can safely handle the sturdy shells.

Materials
- ▲ selection of shells in as many varieties, sizes, and colors possible
- ▲ pan filled with a shallow layer of sand for displaying the shells
- ▲ illustrations of shells and ocean scenes
- ▲ magnifying glasses

Scientific Information
Shells are the homes of some animals (such as mollusks) in the ocean. They vary in type, size, color, and texture. Although you can hear sounds in some shells, the phenomenon is related to the shape of the shell and not, as many children are told, the sound of the ocean. Some shells are really one half of a pair that belong to bivalve animals.

Sequence of Implementation
1. Begin with four or five of the largest shells available that vary in type and color.
2. Add the shallow pan of sand and display some smaller varieties of shells on top of the sand.
3. Add the magnifying glasses.

What to Look For

Some children will pound the shells on the table to find out what sounds are produced.

Some children will compare the shells to the displayed illustrations.

Some children may poke their fingers into the openings of the shells.

Children may talk about previous experiences with shells or the ocean.

Children may hold shells to their ears and try to hear sounds.

Questions to Extend Thinking

Can you find any other shells like this one?

What do you think the animal that lived in this shell might look like?

Modifications

Place tiny shells inside a small magnifying box and add them to the area.

Add water to the sand. Children can press the shells into the wet sand and observe the impressions they make.

Integrated Curriculum Activities

Bury small shells in the sandbox or sensory table and dig for treasures.

Glue small shells as an art activity.

Include the book *Swimmy,* by Leo Lionni, in the reading area.

Consider purchasing a hermit crab for a class pet.

Design a music area for the classroom using shells as instruments (activity 6.15).

Helpful Hint

A basket of shells from a dollar store may contain many of the shells for this display.

2.14 A Walk in the Sand
Shoe Prints

Description
In this display, children use doll shoes and other miniature shoes to make impressions in wet sand. This can be a follow-up to activity 2.13.

Child's Level
This display is appropriate for older preschool and kindergarten children.

Materials
▲ small pan filled with a shallow layer of white sand (about 1½ inches)
▲ doll shoes, shoes from key chains, or baby shoes

Scientific Information
Wet sand responds differently than dry sand. When objects are pressed into wet sand, an impression is made. The impression changes as the sand dries and the sand granules collapse onto each other.

Sequence of Implementation
1. Begin with shoes that have a distinct design on the bottom, such as tennis shoes. Children can quickly draw a relationship between the image on the sole and the one in the sand.
2. Add shoes with a high heel, flat bottomed shoes, and shoes with a small heel. Children notice that shoes with a raised heel produce an impression with a gap between the toe and heel of the shoe.

What to Look For
Children will be fascinated by the impressions shoes make in the sand.

Some children may want to play with the sand. You can direct them to other sand activities or encourage them to press the shoes into the sand.

Some children may want to press their own shoes into the sand.

Questions to Extend Thinking

What makes the design in the sand?

Is there a way to press the shoe so that you only make a heel print?

What has happened to this print? (Point to an area of dried sand.)

Why can't we see the middle of the print this shoe makes? (Point to the shoe with a heel.)

Modification

Add a second pan filled with a different type of sand, such as the kind used in construction or on sidewalks to prevent slipping.

Integrated Curriculum Activities

Plan a shoe print activity that uses paint (activity 5.6).

Include small shoes with playdough (activity 5.22).

Paint the bottom of children's feet and let them make footprints on a roll of shelf paper.

In warm weather, plan other wet sand activities in the outdoor area.

Helpful Hint

Use a pan with high sides to keep the sand from spilling out.

2.15 Search for Hidden Ore
Magnets and Iron Filings

Description

In preparation for this display, mix iron filings in sand. Children use a magnet to search for the iron filings, which are attracted to the magnet. Since this display uses only two substances, iron and sand (a nonmetallic material), children can readily observe that iron is attracted to the magnet.

Child's Level

This display is appropriate for older preschool and kindergarten children.

Materials

▲ a small pan filled with a shallow layer of white sand
▲ iron filings to mix into the sand
▲ small magnetic bingo wands

Scientific Information

Iron is attracted to magnets. Sand particles, which are not iron, are not attracted to magnets.

Sequence of Implementation

1. Begin with a large quantity of iron filings so that the attraction to the magnet will be readily apparent. Be sure to use the label for the iron filings as you talk with children.
2. Reduce the quantity of iron filings so that the search becomes more difficult.

What to Look For

Children may view this as magical since they cannot control whether the iron filings stick to the magnet or not. They always stick.

Children will observe that sand is not attracted to the magnet and will not stick.

Questions to Extend Thinking

What is happening?

What can you do with the magnetic wand?

Modification

Hide other objects in the sand that will not be attracted to the magnetic wand.

Integrated Curriculum Activities

Use Magnastiks, a commercially available toy, as a manipulative activity.

Make cutouts of book characters. Use magnetic tape on the back of them and use when retelling a story.

Helpful Hints

Before you add iron filings, try the magnetic wand to see if your sand already contains some iron. You may be surprised!

Children cannot observe the iron content of such metallic objects as paper clips or tacks. Using magnets with these objects does not help children understand that it is iron, and not all metals, that is attracted to magnets.

2.16 Crazy Climbers
Building on Magnets

Description
Magnets and iron pieces allow children to build structures that would not be possible with standard building materials. Children may experiment with commercial magnet pieces (such as Magnastiks) or with teacher-made pieces cut from a sheet of magnetic material. The pieces in the commercial set are geometric shapes. You can use such items as washers, hexagonal nuts, or coins to trace shapes onto the sheet of magnetic material.

"Magnastiks" pictured here by GEJI.

Child's Level
This display is appropriate for preschool and kindergarten children.

Materials
▲ commercial Magnastiks activity, or teacher-made version as described above
▲ illustrations of metal sculptures or "junk" sculptures from art catalogs

Scientific Information
When a piece of iron comes in contact with a magnet, the iron then becomes magnetized. It remains magnetized as long as it maintains contact with the magnet and for a short period of time thereafter. The magnetized iron can attract other pieces of iron, which then also become magnetized. It is this principle that enables the metallic pieces in this display to adhere to each other in such unusual configurations.

Sequence of Implementation
1. Begin with a selection of 20–25 pieces in triangular, rectangular, and circular shapes.
2. Add the smaller pieces, which may be more difficult for children to handle.

What to Look For

Some children will build flat structures.
Some children will figure out how to balance the shapes in a three-dimensional way.
Some children will construct bridges between the magnets.

Questions to Extend Thinking

What can you do with these pieces?
How can you make a taller structure? (Ask this if the child has not tried a three-dimensional structure.)

Modification

Add other objects containing iron to the activity. Washers and screws are possibilities.

Integrated Curriculum Activities

Plan other magnet experiences in the classroom (activity 2.15).
Use similar building materials that do not involve magnets so that children can compare them.

Helpful Hint

Old art catalogs may be available from a local art gallery or museum. These may be a resource for sculpture illustrations.

2.17 Spin, Spin, Spin
Tops

Description
A collection of interesting tops is a challenge to children. They have to figure out how to make them spin as well as observe the different reactions. Some make music, some draw spiral marks, and some just spin!

Child's Level
This display is most appropriate for older preschool and kindergarten children.

Materials
- ▲ variety of tops from toy and craft stores, odd-lot and dollar stores, and museum shops
- ▲ two trays approximately 9 by 12 inches each
- ▲ illustrations of tops from catalogs

Scientific Information
Tops spin due to gyroscopic motion and centripetal force. A spinning mass wants to maintain its axis of rotation.

Sequence of Implementation
1. Begin with the duplicates of the three varieties of tops that are the easiest to make spin.
2. After one week of exploration, add one or two new types of tops.
3. Add additional tops and remove others. For example, doodle tops or musical tops can replace one of the original display tops.

What to Look For
Many children require an extended period of time for exploration in order to figure out how to make the tops spin.

Some children will have previous experiences with tops and quickly demonstrate spinning the tops for other children.

A few children may discover how to begin spinning a top 6 or 8 inches above the tray and drop it onto the tray where it continues to spin.

Questions to Extend Thinking

What happens if you hold this part of the top to make it spin? (Point to the handle.)

How much longer do you think this top will continue to spin?

Is there a way to make the top spin for a longer time?

Modification

Include rotating laser disk toys from museum shops.

Integrated Curriculum Activities

Plan spin-art as an art activity (activity 5.14).

Include a dance studio in the dramatic play area. Children can spin as they dance.

Helpful Hint

The tray helps contain the tops on the display area.

Machines and Pendulums

Stephen busily hammered bottle caps onto a piece of wood at the woodworking bench. As he finished nailing the last bottle cap, he turned eagerly to the teacher and said, "Look. If I turn one bottle cap, they all move." He had constructed his own set of gears.

▲ ▲ ▲

Angkasa played quietly at the playdough table for a long time. When the teacher came over to check on him, she discovered that he had used the playdough to construct a ramp and a variety of balls. Angkasa rolled each playdough ball down the incline and carefully observed the outcome. He had been experimenting with ramps for several weeks in the science area of his classroom and had now made his own incline out of a completely different medium.

▲ ▲ ▲

Children are fascinated with the properties of machines and pendulums. They eagerly explore the many possibilities created as they experiment with how objects react in relationship to machines and pendulums. They construct important scientific concepts as they observe the results of their actions. Experimenting with machines and pendulums encourages children to think, observe, compare, and discuss.

Teachers' Questions
What are simple machines?

Simple machines are devices that help people lift or move things more easily than by muscle alone. There are six simple machines: the lever, wheel and axle, pulley, inclined plane, wedge, and screw.

▲ ***Lever***—A lever is a bar with a support, called a *fulcrum*. The lever is used to pry things open or lift heavy objects a short distance.

- ▲ **Wheel and Axle**—The wheel and axle is a modification of the lever. A load attached to the axle, or *spindle*, can be lifted much more easily by turning the larger wheel than by turning the axle itself. A doorknob and a crank are examples of wheel and axles.
- ▲ **Pulley**—A pulley is a wheel with a grooved rim through which a rope is passed. A pulley enables a person to move an object by pulling in a direction opposite to the direction the object is to be moved. Through the use of a pulley, a heavy object can be lifted up by pulling down on a rope. Pulling down is considerably easier than pulling up.
- ▲ **Inclined Plane**—An inclined plane is a flat surface that slants or slopes. Heavy objects can be more easily moved by pushing them up an inclined plane than by lifting them.
- ▲ **Wedge**—The wedge is an adaptation of the inclined plane. It is actually two inclined planes joined together. Wedges are useful in cutting or splitting things. Knives and axes are examples.
- ▲ **Screw**—The screw is a spiral inclined plane. It can lift a heavy object easily, as when a car jack that utilizes a crank lifts an automobile.

Why should teachers include simple machines in the science curriculum?

Simple machines encourage scientific exploration and the construction of physical knowledge. With simple machines, children can perform a physical action, such as pulling the rope on a pulley or rolling objects down an incline, and observe the results. This encourages them to create many relationships involving the physical properties of materials. Trying out many possibilities helps children become more flexible thinkers.

What scientific principles emerge as children experiment with simple machines?

Children discover that simple machines make work easier. Children construct additional scientific knowledge that is specific to each type of machine. The specific scientific principles are discussed under the "Scientific Information" headings in each activity.

What is a pendulum?

A pendulum is a weight suspended from a fixed point so that it can swing back and forth. Although the pendulum is not a simple machine, children experiment with pendulums in the same way that they experiment with simple machines. For example, children can use both pendulums and inclines to knock down blocks or other objects.

What do children learn from experimenting with pendulums?

Children learn several different concepts from experimenting with pendulums:

▲ They discover that the path of the pendulum is curved rather than straight.

▲ They construct relationships between the length of the rope on the pendulum and the arc of its swing.

▲ They learn that the weight of the pendulum affects what it can and cannot knock down.

Children initially expect the pendulum to behave like a ball or similar object that they have thrown or rolled. If the pendulum fails to reach the object the child is trying to knock down, the child typically responds by trying to throw or swing the pendulum harder. It takes much experimentation for children to finally realize that the pendulum always follows an arc-shaped path. Increasing the force used to swing the pendulum does not change this fact.

How do simple machines and pendulums encourage children to use the scientific process?

As children experiment with simple machines and pendulums they form hypotheses, observe and compare results, classify, measure, draw inferences, and communicate their observations. These are all aspects of the scientific process. Teachers can facilitate this process through the comments they make and the questions they ask children as they interact with the materials. Suggestions for questions to encourage scientific thinking are included with each activity in this chapter.

Where can teachers find simple machines?

Some simple machines, such as pulleys and levers, are commercially available. Teachers can also create simple machines with inexpensive materials that are readily available. See the individual activities for suggestions.

How can teachers make a pendulum?

Teachers can create a pendulum by suspending a weighted object from a small A-frame, such as an infant gym, or from a 6-inch blunt hook inserted into a pegboard divider or the back of a shelf. Teachers can also construct small pendulum frames. Illustrations and instructions for creating pendulums accompany each pendulum activity.

What is the best way to display simple machines and pendulums?

A science area in the classroom, which includes a low bench or small table to hold the materials, is ideal. The area should be large enough to accommodate several children to encourage shared experiences. A bulletin board, pegboard divider, or the back of a shelf provides an area for mounting pictures and relevant print.

How long should each activity remain in the classroom?

Two to three weeks is typical, although additions or modifications to the area may occur several times during this period. Children need ample time to explore the many possibilities related to the activities. For example, children might initially use a pendulum to knock down blocks. During the second week, the teacher might shorten the rope on the pendulum so children could experience how this change affects the outcome. During the third week, children might adjust the rope length themselves.

What is the teacher's role?

The teacher's role is to facilitate the children's construction of knowledge. This begins with a carefully designed activity that encourages children to experiment and explore and to observe and communicate the results. Teachers can encourage this process through well-timed comments and questions that stimulate thinking. In addition, as teachers observe children interacting with the materials, they can plan and introduce additions or modifications that extend the thinking process.

Integrating science activities throughout the curriculum is another way for teachers to facilitate and expand the construction of knowledge. For example, after children have experimented with pendulums in the science area, the teacher might plan an art activity where children paint with pendulums (activity 5.11).

How can teachers assess the development of children's scientific knowledge?

Teachers can carefully observe children as they interact with the materials, and they can ask pertinent questions to delve into their thinking. Teachers can record the information anecdotally or use an assessment tool such as the one found in appendix A.6. Suggestions for questions to ask and what to look for as children interact with materials are included with each activity.

What are children's levels of thinking when exploring the physical properties of objects?

Based on Piaget's writings, Constance Kamii describes four levels of thinking when children act on objects.[1]

1. ***Acting on objects and seeing how they react.*** This is a stage of free exploration with no intention on the child's part to produce a particular outcome. Babies engage in this type of behavior, and so do children when they initially explore new materials.

2. ***Acting on objects to produce a desired effect.*** At this level children exhibit intentional behavior. They have a definite outcome in mind as they interact with materials. Late in the first year, babies begin to show intentional behavior, such as dropping a cup to watch it fall. Young children also act on objects to produce a desired effect, especially after they have had a period of time for free exploration.

3. ***Becoming aware of how one produced the desired effect.*** Four- and five-year-old children are often skillful at producing specific results when interacting with objects; however, they are not able to accurately and completely describe how they produced the result. This level of thinking is not reached until much later.

4. ***Explaining causes.*** Since young children cannot explain how they produced a desired effect, they certainly cannot explain the causes of most phenomena. This is why understanding scientific explanations is impossible for young children, although they are often required to memorize them in school science curriculums.

What questions should teachers ask based on children's levels of thinking?

The type of question is an outgrowth of the child's interactions with the materials.

1. If the child is ***acting on objects to see how they react***, or if the child is hanging back and not interacting with the materials, then the teacher can ask open-ended questions that encourage play and experimentation.

> "What can you do with these objects?"
> "I wonder what this can do."

2. If the child appears to be ***acting on objects to produce a desired effect***, or if the child has already had a long period of free exploration, the teacher can ask questions that focus thinking on possible outcomes.

> "How can you move the basket to your side of the pulley frame?"
> "What will happen if you shorten the rope on the pendulum?"

3. Although research indicates that young children will not be able to ***describe completely how they produced the desired effect***, the teacher might occasionally draw the child's thinking along those lines.

> "Could you tell John what you had to do to knock over all those blocks?"
> "What did you do to the ramp to make the car roll faster?"

4. While asking young children to ***explain causes*** is generally fruitless, sometimes teachers interject such questions to encourage children to ponder possibilities. Teachers can expect magical answers to this type of question; therefore, they should most often gear questioning to levels of thinking that are closer to the child's developmental level.

> "I wonder why the water doesn't come out of this hole. What do you think?"

Endnotes

1. Constance Kamii and Rheta DeVries, *Physical Knowledge in Preschool Education* (New York: Prentice-Hall, 1978) 48–50.

Machine and Pendulum Activities

3.1 Ramps and Things
Inclined Plane

Description
The physical properties of objects affect how they move down an incline, or ramp. In this activity, children experiment with rolling a variety of objects down a wide ramp and observe the results.

Child's Level
This activity is appropriate for either preschool or kindergarten children.

Materials
▲ ramp (approximately 22 by 11 by 5 inches), made from a hollow wooden block or sturdy cardboard
▲ a variety of small objects to roll down the ramp, such as small balls, a 1-inch cube, spools, a curtain ring, a film canister, and a cardboard tube

Scientific Information
Rounded objects roll better than objects with edges.

Sequence of Implementation
1. Start with objects that roll so that the children can first focus on the incline and not be placed in immediate disequilibrium by objects that don't roll. (Disequilibrium is a discrepancy between what children think and what they observe.)
2. Add some objects that don't roll, such as a cube or small box.
3. Finally, include some materials that respond uniquely, such as a tube that is larger at one end than at the other.

What to Look For
Children may compare how various objects roll down the ramp.
Some children may roll the objects in different ways to see how far they can roll.
Some children may initially play with the balls in a familiar way, such as throwing them, until redirected.

Questions to Extend Thinking

What can you do with these things to make them go?
What happens if you put the ball at this place on the ramp?
How can you stop them from rolling down?
Why doesn't this one roll?
Which object rolls the fastest?

Modification

Include an observation sheet or booklet so that children can write down or dictate their observations and conclusions.

Integrated Curriculum Activities

Encourage children to collect additional materials to experiment with on the ramp.
Include ramps in the gross-motor areas, such as inclines to walk up and down, slides, and wedge mats for rolling and tumbling.
Add incline activities, such as marble tracks, to the manipulative area.

Helpful Hint

Begin with balls that don't look like children's play equipment. Children may be less likely to throw them.

3.2 Ramp Race
Inclined Plane

Description
The slope of an incline, or how steep it is, affects the speed of objects rolling down it. This activity has two ramps with different slopes. Children can roll small cars down the ramps and compare their speeds. This is a good follow-up to activity 3.1.

Child's Level
This activity is appropriate for either preschool or kindergarten children.

Materials
▲ two ramps made from unit blocks, one 6 inches tall and the other 3 inches tall
▲ small cars to roll down the ramps
▲ other objects, such as balls, cubes, tubes, and spools

Scientific Information
Objects roll down a ramp with a steep slope faster than one with a more gradual incline.

Sequence of Implementation
1. Start with two identical cars, including color, so children focus on the differences in the ramps and not the differences between the cars.
2. Add a variety of types of cars so that children can experiment with the effect the varying slopes have on a variety of cars.
3. Include the other objects for experimentation.

What to Look For
Children may race the cars down the ramps.
Some children may roll the cars in different ways to alter their speeds.
Many children will discover that cars and other objects roll faster down the steeper slope.

Questions to Extend Thinking
Which car do you think will get to the bottom first?
Why do you think this car went faster?
Where should I put my car to make it go slowly?

Modification
Write down the children's predictions before they race the cars.
They can then check their hypotheses.

Integrated Curriculum Activities
Try a painting activity that involves slope, such as marble painting (activity 5.7).
Encourage children to build their own ramps in the block and
manipulative areas.

Helpful Hint
Place a tray under the ramps to keep objects from rolling across
the floor.

3.3 Adjustable Ramp
Inclined Plane

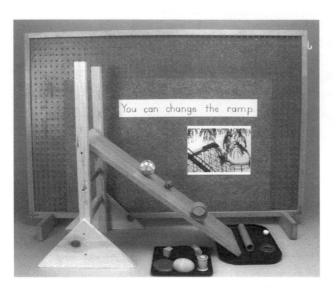

Thanks to Kim Rioux for her design of this ramp.

Description
In this activity, children can alter the slope (steepness) of a wide incline and observe the effect on a variety of objects that they roll down the ramp. The ramp is made from a piece of ¾-inch shelving approximately 28 inches long and 9½ inches wide. Two strips of ½-inch thick wood, 1½ inches wide and 8¾ inches long, are screwed across the width of one end of the ramp. A gap between these strips of wood enables children to hook it over the dowels on a ladder frame. The ladder frame is made from 1½-inch square wood, 28 inches long. Drill holes in the wood to hold three dowels, ¾ inch in diameter and 12 inches long. Triangular braces support the bottom of the ladder. Children can attach the ramp to any of the three levels of the ladder.

Child's Level
This activity is most appropriate for older preschool or kindergarten children.

Materials
- ▲ adjustable ramp, as described above
- ▲ small cars and other objects to roll down the ramp

Scientific Information
The greater the slope of an incline, the faster objects move down it.

Sequence of Implementation
1. Start by rolling only the cars down the ramp so that the children can focus on the effect of slope on moving objects rather than on the differences among the objects.
2. Add other objects to roll down the ramp, including some that do not typically roll, such as a rectangular table block.

What to Look For
At first, children may be primarily interested in manipulating the
ramp.
Children may compare how changing the steepness of the incline
affects the way the objects behave.
Some children may experiment with rolling objects up the ramp.

Questions to Extend Thinking
What can you do with this board and frame?
What do you think will happen when you roll the objects if we
raise the ramp to this rung of the ladder?
Where should I put the ramp to make my car move slowly?
Is there any way to adjust the ramp so that this block rolls down?

Modification
Place film canisters or small blocks at the bottom of the ramp for
children to knock down. This encourages children to focus on the
path of each rolling object.

Integrated Curriculum Activities
Include adjustable ramps in the gross-motor areas for children to
experiment walking up and down.
Dip objects in paint and roll them down a ramp to make trails
(activity 5.7).

Helpful Hint
Construct smaller versions of the adjustable ramp if the size
described above is too cumbersome for younger children.

3.4 Bump, Bump, Over the Hump
Inclined Plane

Description
This modification of activity 3.1 gives children an opportunity to observe what happens when an object that is moving down an incline meets an impediment. Children can place strips of molding of various heights across the ramp and observe how the objects rolling down the ramp react when they hit the molding. Children can also vary the location of the molding on the ramp and observe the results.

Child's Level
This activity is most appropriate for older preschool and kindergarten children.

Materials
- ▲ ramp (approximately 22 by 11 by 5 inches), made from a hollow wooden block or sturdy cardboard
- ▲ strips of wood molding long enough to go across the width of the ramp
- ▲ small brackets to hold the molding onto the ramp
- ▲ a variety of small objects to roll down the ramp, such as small cars, wooden beads, spools, cardboard tubes, and small blocks

Scientific Information
Objects that are moving down an incline and meet an obstruction change their motion based on the height of the impediment and their speed when they encounter it. If the obstacle is low, the moving object may slow down and continue over it; however, a higher obstruction may stop the moving object altogether. An increase in speed may allow an object to continue moving over an obstruction that stopped its progress at a slower speed.

Sequence of Implementation
1. Start with small cars and one size of molding. This allows children to focus on the movement of the cars as they hit the molding and to move the molding to various locations along the ramp.
2. Introduce molding of various heights for children to experiment with on the ramp.
3. Add a variety of objects for children to observe as they hit the molding.

What to Look For
Children will roll objects down the ramp and watch what happens when they meet an impediment.

Children will change the molding to observe the results.

Children will experiment with moving the molding strips to various locations along the ramp and compare the results.

Questions to Extend Thinking
What do you think will happen to the car when it hits the molding?

What happens if you put a bigger piece of molding on the ramp?

What happens when the car is rolling slowly and hits the molding?

What happens when the molding is near the top of the ramp?

Modification
After children have experimented with the molding strips on this ramp, try adding a similar obstruction to the adjustable ramp (activity 3.3). Children can see how the height of a ramp affects how objects react when they hit an obstruction.

Integrated Curriculum Activities
Put cars in the block area. Children may want to create ramps and obstructions of their own.

Let children roll cars and other small vehicles in paint and use them to make tracks. They can compare the size of the tracks made by the various wheels (activity 5.10).

Construct a ramp out of hollow wooden blocks for children to ride tricycles up and down.

Helpful Hint
Glue small brackets to the ramp to hold the strips of molding.

3.5 Flip-Flop and Drop
Inclined Plane

Description

In this activity, cars or marbles reverse direction as they drop through a series of overlapping ramps. One of the ramps is commercially available. You can make the other by gluing and nailing 4-inch long pieces of counter molding to a wooden board (8 by 16 inches) at an angle, as pictured. Nail the lip of each segment of counter molding to the backboard. Then glue a second strip of molding, with the lip to the outside, onto each ramp segment. This outer ridge helps keep the marbles on the ramps. Wood footings at the bottom of the frame allow it to stand up.

"Race Way" pictured here by Fisher Price.

Child's Level

This activity is most appropriate for older preschool or kindergarten children.

Materials

▲ either or both of the ramp mazes pictured
▲ cars, marbles, or small balls to roll down the ramps

Scientific Information

Objects moving from one incline to another change direction relative to the downward slope of the incline. Cars rotate (or flip) as they fall off the edge of an incline because one part of the car is supported and the other is not.

Sequence of Implementation

1. Start with the car maze, if available, since the cars are a little easier to handle than the marbles and are very intriguing to children.
2. Add a second maze with marbles so that children can compare how the marbles fall through the maze with how the cars react. If a second maze is not available, substitute marbles for cars in the first maze.
3. Add additional objects for experimentation. Small balls, beads, or bottle caps are possibilities.

What to Look For

Children seem to want to watch the objects drop through the mazes over and over.

Children may line up several marbles or cars and watch the sequence of their arrival at the bottom of the maze.

Questions to Extend Thinking

How can you make these things move through the maze?

What happens to the car when it goes from this ramp to this ramp?

If I line up these three marbles, which one will get to the bottom first?

Modification

Elevate the maze on a block so children can catch the objects as they roll off.

Integrated Curriculum Activities

Include marble tracks in the manipulative area.

Put clear plastic tubing and marbles in the water table (activity 4.5).

Attach a piece of clear tubing with a bead inside to a teeter-totter. Close the ends of the tube. Children can watch the movement of the bead as they move up and down on the teeter-totter (activity 8.9).

Helpful Hint

Experiment with the positioning of the ramps before you permanently attach them to the backboard.

3.6 Rough and Smooth
Inclined Plane

Description
The surface of an incline affects how objects roll down it. This activity has two ramps that are identical except for one attribute: one ramp has a smooth wood surface and the other has a coarse sandpaper surface.

Child's Level
This activity is appropriate for either preschool or kindergarten children.

Materials
▲ two ramps made from unit blocks or heavy cardboard, with sandpaper glued to one ramp
▲ small cars or other objects to roll down the ramps

Scientific Information
Objects move more slowly down an incline with a rough surface than down a smooth one due to the increased friction.

Sequence of Implementation
1. Start with two identical cars, including color, so that children can focus on the differences in the surfaces of the ramps rather than the properties of the objects.
2. Add a variety of types of cars so that children can notice a similar effect on them as they move between the surfaces of the two inclines.
3. Introduce other objects, such as blocks, beads, or spools, for experimentation.

What to Look For
Children may feel the two surfaces and then compare how cars or other objects move down them.
Children may alter how they roll objects on the sandpaper ramp in order to help the objects move faster.
Some children may experiment with rolling objects up the inclines.
Older children may wish to record their observations.

Questions to Extend Thinking
Are there any differences between the two ramps?
How do the cars move on these two ramps?
Why did this car get to the bottom first?

Modification
Include additional ramps with other types of surfaces, such as cloth or sponge.

Integrated Curriculum Activities
Provide a variety of materials for collages in the art area.
Include vehicles and material samples in the block area so that
    children can construct their own ramps with various surfaces.

Helpful Hint
Place a tray under the ramps to contain the rolling objects.

3.7 Open and Shut
Lever

Description
In this activity, children construct knowledge about how a lever can be used to pry open lids. Children discover that lids which they couldn't lift with their fingers alone can be moved with this simple machine.

Child's Level
This activity is most appropriate for older preschool or kindergarten children.

Materials
▲ boxes, jars, or cans with lids that can be pried open (cocoa boxes, paint cans, etc.)
▲ spoon, screwdriver, and quarter to use as levers
▲ large pompoms to put into the cans

Scientific Information
Levers help people use their strength more effectively so work is easier.

Sequence of Implementation
1. Start with a variety of containers and several spoons for children to use as levers. This simplifies the activity by allowing children to figure out how to open the containers with just one implement.
2. Add other objects to use as levers, such as a screwdriver and a quarter. Children can discover which is the easiest to use.

What to Look For
Children will experiment in order to learn how to pry off the lids.
Some children may wish to put objects into the cans.
Children may compare how well the various implements work in opening the lids.

Questions to Extend Thinking

How can you use the spoon to open the can?
What happens if you use the other end of the spoon?
Can you use any of these things to open the lids?
What did you do to make the screwdriver work?
Which implement works the best for opening the containers?

Modification

Provide three sizes of screwdrivers. Children can experiment with them to determine how the length of the lever affects the ease of use.

Integrated Curriculum Activities

Put implements such as Popsicle sticks in the block area for
    children to use as levers.
Paint with various lengths of paintbrushes. Paintbrushes are also
    levers.
Use shovels in the sandbox. They are another form of lever.
Plan a shoe store for the dramatic play area. Include shoe horns
    and empty shoe polish cans that have a small lever attached to
    the side for opening the lid.

Helpful Hint

One gallon paint cans are hard for children to open because of their wide circumference. Start with small lids for earlier success.

3.8 Pounding and Prying
Wedge and Lever

Description
In this activity, children hammer golf tees into Styrofoam and then pry them out with spoons. The golf tee functions as a type of wedge, while the hammer and spoon are levers.

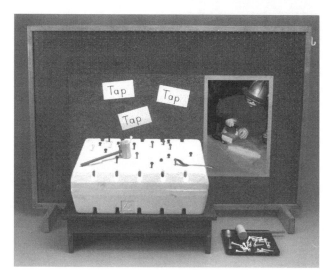

Child's Level
This activity is appropriate for either preschool or kindergarten children.

Materials
▲ Styrofoam sheets, at least 2 inches thick
▲ wooden or plastic golf tees
▲ two wooden hammers
▲ two spoons

Scientific Information
The wedge and the lever help focus our energy to make work easier. In this activity, the golf tee is a wedge that splits the Styrofoam easier than a blunt object would. The hammer and spoon are different forms of levers. While the hammer allows us to push the golf tees into the Styrofoam easier than by hand alone, the spoon enables us to pry them out, which is difficult by finger strength alone.

Sequence of Implementation
None required.

What to Look For
Children quickly become adept at hammering the golf tees into the Styrofoam.
Some children will learn to use the spoons to pry the golf tees out of the Styrofoam.

Questions to Extend Thinking
How can you get the pegs into the Styrofoam?
How can you get them out?
How difficult is it to push the pegs into the Styrofoam with your fingers?

Modification
Switch to real nails and wood when you feel your class is ready.

Integrated Curriculum Activities
Sing hammering songs at group time. See *More Than Singing,* by
  Sally Moomaw, activity 7.3.
Hammer golf tees into other materials, such as playdough.
Set up the dramatic play area as a construction site with hard
  hats, toy tools, and large blocks for building.

Helpful Hint
Ask parents to save Styrofoam packing material for this activity.

3.9 Heavy or Light, Check the Height

Lever

Description

A balance is a type of lever with the fulcrum in the center. In this activity, children can compare objects that look similar but have different weights by observing their effect on the balance.

"Rocker Scale" pictured here by Invicta Plastics Ltd.

Child's Level

This activity is appropriate for either preschool or kindergarten children.

Materials

▲ balance
▲ pairs of objects that look similar but differ in weight, such as an Osage orange and a tennis ball or fresh and dried gourds

Scientific Information

Gravity exerts more pull on the heavier side of the balance than the lighter side, which causes the heavier side to go down. Since both sides are connected by the lever, when the heavier side goes down, the lighter side must go up.

Sequence of Implementation

1. Start with one pair of objects that look alike but have different weights. This will allow children to focus on the properties of the balance.
2. Add other objects for comparison.
3. Change to one type of material, such as buckeyes, so children can observe the effect of quantity on the behavior of the balance.

What to Look For

Until they have had many experiences with the balance, many of the children will label the side that is up as heavier.

Children will experiment with putting objects on the balance and taking them off. Many materials may find their way to the balance!

Some children may try to keep the balance level, especially in step 3.

Questions to Extend Thinking

What happens when you put these things on the balance?

Which side do you think is heavier?

How can you add these buckeyes to the balance and still keep it level?

What makes the balance move?

How can I make this side go up?

Modification

Once children have had experience with the balance, create disequilibrium by supplying an object that is large but lightweight (such as balsa wood) and an object that is small but heavy (such as a lead weight).

Integrated Curriculum Activities

Include teeter-totters in the gross-motor areas.

Let children weigh themselves and compare the results.

Add a scale to the dramatic play area for weighing fruits and vegetables.

Helpful Hint

Some balances only move a short distance before they hit the ground. If this is the case, elevate the balance by setting it on a block so that children can see a wider range of movement.

3.10 Corn Plucking
Double Lever

Description
Children are enthralled with using tweezers to pluck dried kernels of corn from the cob. Tweezers are a double lever.

Child's Level
This activity is most appropriate for older preschool or kindergarten children due to the level of fine-motor skill required.

Materials
▲ dried ears of corn
▲ several pairs of tweezers

Scientific Information
Tweezers form a double lever with the fulcrum at the joint where the two bars meet. It is easier to remove kernels of corn from the cob with tweezers than with fingers alone, especially when the kernels are packed tightly together on the cob.

Sequence of Implementation
1. Start with large ears of corn. They are easier for children to handle.
2. Add smaller ears of corn.
3. Switch to another material, such as dried sunflowers.

What to Look For
Children may need time to experiment with the tweezers before they can coordinate them.
Some children will attempt to remove the kernels from the cob with their fingers.
Some children will use the tweezers to pry the kernels rather than to grasp and pull them.
Children may pull the kernels off the cob with their fingers once there is an empty space on the cob.

Questions to Extend Thinking
How can you get the kernels of corn off the cob?
Is it easier to pull with your fingers or the tweezers? Why?

Modification
Vary the type of tweezer. Some are manipulated in a manner
similar to scissors.

Integrated Curriculum Activities
Read books about corn, such as *Raccoons and Ripe Corn,* by Jim
    Arnosky, and *The Popcorn Book,* by Tomie de Paola.
Grind the corn once the children have removed the kernels
    (activities 3.11 and 3.12).
Use corn kernels for collages.
Put dried corn in the sensory table with scoops and buckets.
Plant corn kernels and observe the results.

Helpful Hint
Place a small basket or bowl in the science area for children to
use to collect the kernels of corn.

3.11 Mortar and Pestle
Lever

Description
Many cultures use some sort of mortar and pestle for grinding grain. The pestle, like the hammer in activity 3.8, is a type of lever. In this activity, children can grind dried kernels of corn by pounding them. Children can also observe the changes in the corn when it is crushed into a powder.

Child's Level
This activity is most appropriate for older preschool or kindergarten children.

Materials
▲ mortar and pestle, which can be purchased, or a wooden bowl and wooden dowel (approximately 1 inch in diameter and 6 inches long)
▲ dried kernels of corn

Scientific Information
Corn kernels can be ground into a powder if enough force is applied. The pestle channels muscle strength effectively so that corn can be ground by pounding it with a device such as the pestle or a rock.

Sequence of Implementation
None required.

What to Look For
Children enjoy pulverizing the corn and observing the result.
Some children will be more interested in stirring the corn than grinding it.
Some children may have difficulty crushing the corn, especially at first.

Questions to Extend Thinking
What can you do with the mortar and pestle and the corn?
What happens to the corn if you pound it?
How did you get the corn to turn into powder?
What else can you think of that looks like this cornmeal?
What could we do with this cornmeal?

Modification
Try grinding other types of grain once children have had experience with the corn.

Integrated Curriculum Activities
Cook with cornmeal. Tortillas and cornbread are possibilities.
Read books about cornmeal, such as *The Tortilla Factory,* by Gary
 Paulsen, and *The Story of the Milky Way, A Cherokee Tale*, by
 Joseph Bruchac and Gayle Ross.
Use dried corn on the cob and cobs stripped of their corn as
 painting implements.

Helpful Hint
The corn kernels often go flying out of the mortar as children
pound them. To eliminate this problem, cover the corn with a
paper towel or thin cloth before the children begin pounding.

3.12 Corn Grinder
Wheel and Axle, Screw

Description
Children find the corn grinder easier to use than the mortar and pestle. They put kernels of corn into the grinder and turn a crank, which is a wheel and axle. A screw advances the corn until it is crushed. It emerges in a powdery form through small holes at the end of the grinder. Children find the entire process fascinating.

What happens to the corn in the grain mill?

"Grain Mill" pictured here by Back to Basics.

Child's Level
This activity is most appropriate for older preschool or kindergarten children.

Materials
▲ hand-operated grain mill, available through health food stores
▲ kernels of dried corn

Scientific Information
A wheel and axle can be used for turning a screw. The screw moves the corn forward until it can be crushed. These simple machines allow the corn to be crushed with much less effort than by pounding. Children know this if they have done the mortar and pestle activity (3.11)!

Sequence of Implementation
1. Start with dried corn for grinding. Children can see a dramatic difference as it emerges from the mill.
2. After children have had many experiences grinding corn, try other grains, such as rice.

What to Look For
Children will spend endless amounts of time grinding the corn.
Children will watch the corn as it emerges from the end of the grinder.
Children will compare the state of the corn as it enters the grinder with its state as it emerges.

Questions to Extend Thinking
How can you use this machine to grind the corn?
What is happening to the corn?
What is another way to grind the corn into powder?

Modification
Children can explore the entire sequence of making flour from grain. They can first pluck the kernels from dried corn cobs (activity 3.10) and then grind it using both the mortar and pestle method (activity 3.11) and the grain mill. Children can then compare their cornmeal with commercial cornmeal and then make cornbread.

Integrated Curriculum Activities
As a cooking activity, use hand-turned meat grinders to grind ingredients for ham or egg salad.

Use garlic presses with playdough. Children can watch how the playdough changes as it is forced through the press in a manner similar to how the corn is pressed through the grinder.

Read *Pancakes, Pancakes,* by Eric Carle. It emphasizes the sequence of going from grain to flour.

Helpful Hint
Be sure to supervise the children when they are using the mill to be certain they do not hurt their fingers in the grinder.

3.13 Pulling Down, Going Up
Vertical Pulley

Description
By using a vertical pulley, children discover that they can move objects up by actually pulling down. The pulley is attached to a pegboard divider or the back of a shelf. A platform, also attached to the pegboard, serves as a ledge or "tree house." This may motivate children to use the pulley to move objects up to the platform.

Use the pulley to help you move.

Child's Level
This activity is appropriate for either preschool or kindergarten children.

Materials
- ▲ pulley (as pictured), attached to a 6-inch hook on a pegboard divider, with a small bucket at the bottom of the pulley rope
- ▲ bird feeder, or other small platform, that can be attached to the pegboard divider
- ▲ small objects to transfer up to the platform

Scientific Information
It is easier to move objects upward by pulling down than by pulling up. A pulley makes this possible.

Sequence of Implementation
1. Start with 1-inch cubes to lift with the pulley so children focus on the pulley and not the uniqueness of the objects.
2. Add a variety of interesting objects to lift, such as small animals, dollhouse furniture, or small toy people.
3. Switch to objects with very different weights so children can compare how the weight of the object affects how hard they have to pull.

What to Look For
Children will experiment with raising objects by pulling down on the rope.
Some children, especially at first, will try to pull up on the rope to raise the objects.

Questions to Extend Thinking

How can you get these things up to the platform?
What happens if you pull on this part of the rope?
Why does the bucket go up when you are pulling down?
Which object is the hardest to lift?

Modification

Add a second pulley to form a double pulley. This decreases the amount of strength needed to raise the objects.

Integrated Curriculum Activities

Include a vertical pulley in a gross-motor area after the children have had experiences with the small pulley (see activity 8.4).

Read books about tree houses, such as *Wish I Had a Big, Big Tree,* by Satoru Sato.

Put buckets and water or sand in the sensory table. Children can discover how hard it is to lift the buckets.

Helpful Hint

Attach a bead to the pulley rope on the side of the wheel opposite the side with the bucket. This keeps the bucket from slamming down onto the bench when children let go of the rope.

3.14 Pulling Left, Moving Right
Horizontal Pulley

Description
The horizontal pulley allows children to explore the possibilities for reversal of direction when moving a load. Two pulleys are tied to 6-inch hooks at each end of a pegboard divider or the back of a shelf. Children discover that when they pull the rope in one direction, the load moves in the opposite direction.

Send a shoe to your friend.

Child's Level
This activity is appropriate for either preschool or kindergarten children.

Materials
- ▲ two pulleys connected by rope, with the ends tied to each other to form a continuous loop
- ▲ pegboard divider or the back of a shelf with 6-inch hooks at either end for holding the pulleys
- ▲ small bucket attached to the pulley rope
- ▲ small objects to move with the pulley

Scientific Information
Pulleys enable you to pull in one direction in order to move a load in the opposite direction.

Sequence of Implementation
1. Start with familiar objects for children to move, such as 1-inch cubes. This allows them to focus on the properties of the pulley rather than the uniqueness of the objects.
2. Switch to more unusual objects, such as tiny shoes or shells, to stimulate further interest in the pulley.
3. Provide objects of varying weights so that children can explore the effect this has on the amount of force needed to pull the rope.

What to Look For

Many children will pull the rope in the direction they want the object to move and be surprised when it moves the opposite way.

Children will construct which way to pull the rope in order to get the object to move in the direction they desire.

Two children may pull in opposite directions and have to negotiate with one another in order to get the object to move.

Questions to Extend Thinking

How can you move the bucket?

What do I have to do to move the bucket over here?

Why did the bucket move this way when you pulled that way?

What happens if you pull the rope in this direction?

Modification

Add a second pulley to create a double pulley. This decreases the amount of strength needed to move the objects.

Integrated Curriculum Activities

Incorporate a large horizontal pulley into a gross-motor area after the children have had experience with the small pulley (see activity 8.3).

Plan a math activity where one child decides how many objects are to be transferred by the pulley and another child fills the order. See *More Than Counting*, by Sally Moomaw and Brenda Hieronymus, activity 7.13.

Helpful Hint

Add a small piece of colored tape to the rope to help children visualize which direction the rope is moving.

3.15 Round and Round and Round
Moveable Gears

Description
Many versions of moveable gears are commercially available. Moveable gears enable children to discover how gears behave when interlocked versus when they do not touch another gear.

"Busy Gears" pictured here by Playskool.

Child's Level
This activity is appropriate for either preschool or kindergarten children.

Materials
▲ moveable gear set with board to mount them on

Scientific Information
Gears enable us to transfer movement along a series of interlocking wheels by turning just one. They also change the direction of rotation. For example, if one gear is turned clockwise, the next interlocking gear turns counterclockwise.

Sequence of Implementation
1. Start with all round gears.
2. Add an oval gear if one is available. This gear behaves very differently from the round gears and provides a new challenge.

What to Look For
Many children will randomly place the gears, turn them, and observe the results.

At first children will not understand that the gears have to interlock in order to turn together.

Some children will experiment with a variety of specific gear placements.

Children may repeat specific gear arrangements many times in order to see if the results are always the same.

Questions to Extend Thinking

What can you do with these gears?
How can you get this gear to move without touching it?
If I turn this gear this way, which way will this gear turn?
Is there a way to get all of the gears to move by turning just one?

Modification

Add rubber bands to the gear assembly. Children can experiment with connecting gears in a different way and observe the results.

Integrated Curriculum Activities

Put water wheels or water gears in the sensory table (activities 4.3 and 4.4).
Allow children to experiment with nailing bottle caps to wood in the woodworking area. Some may choose to interlock them as gears.
Add building toys that have gears to the manipulative area.

Helpful Hint

If possible, include at least two sets of gears in the science area. They tend to be very popular.

3.16 Round and Round, Up and Down
Vertical Gears

Description
This activity gives children the opportunity to experiment with gears in a vertical position. The gear structures are made from commercial building sets.

"Gearopolis" pictured here by Discovery Toys. "Gears, Gears, Gears" pictured here by Learning Resources.

Child's Level
This activity is most appropriate for older preschool or kindergarten children.

Materials
▲ gear building set

Scientific Information
Gears can be assembled in a vertical as well as horizontal position. Gears enable us to transfer movement along a series of inter-locking wheels by turning just one.

Sequence of Implementation
1. Start with an already constructed frame to hold several gears, as pictured. This gives children the chance to visualize and interact with vertical and horizontal gears.
2. Leave the existing gear assembly, but add additional gear and frame pieces so children can construct their own gears.
3. Remove the pre-existing gear assembly so children are encouraged to try a variety of gear configurations.

What to Look For
Children will turn the gears and watch the results.
Children will experiment by moving the gears to other positions.
Some children will build their own gear assemblies.

Questions to Extend Thinking
What happens when you turn this gear?
How can you make this gear turn?
How could you use these pieces to build a gear assembly?
Can you build the gears so there are more going upward?

Modification
Combine the gear set with other building materials so children can design more elaborate structures.

Integrated Curriculum Activities
Add water wheels or water gears to the sensory table (activities 4.3 and 4.4).
Older children may wish to experiment with cutting gears out of plastic lids and nailing them to wood.

Helpful Hint
Ask parents for donations of broken appliances that have visible gears for children to examine. Clocks, watches, and telephones are some examples.

3.17 Wrecking Ball
Pendulum

Description
This activity allows children to discover some of the properties of a pendulum as they use it to try to knock down blocks. Mount the pendulum frame on a ½-thick plywood base, 18 by 12 inches. Make the sides of the frame from ¾-inch wood, 16 by 1½ inches. Make the top from ¾-inch wood, 12 by 1½ inches. Screw the frame together and suspend the pendulum weight (a wooden ball) from a screw eye.

Pendulum designed by Melissa Hattersley.

Child's Level
This activity is appropriate for either preschool or kindergarten children.

Materials
▲ pendulum frame, as described above
▲ table blocks to knock down with the pendulum

Scientific Information
The pendulum moves in an arc-shaped path. The distance it can swing depends on the length of the rope attached to the weight.

Sequence of Implementation
1. Begin with several small table blocks for the children to knock down with the pendulum.
2. Once children have become adept at targeting with the pendulum, shorten the rope to cause disequilibrium and encourage further experimentation.
3. With older children, move the pendulum off center to stimulate further thinking.

What to Look For
Children may require a substantial period of experimentation to construct the knowledge of where to place the blocks so that the pendulum can reach them.
Some children will try to throw the pendulum harder if it does not reach the blocks.

Questions to Extend Thinking

Can you knock over the blocks with the pendulum?

Why won't the blocks fall down?

How many blocks can you knock over by just releasing the pendulum once?

What happens if you release the pendulum from this spot?

What did you have to do to knock down all the blocks?

Modification

Substitute film canisters for table blocks. They respond somewhat differently when struck by the pendulum.

Integrated Curriculum Activities

Paint with the pendulum (see activity 5.11).

Read books about construction and knocking down buildings, such as *Bam, Bam, Bam,* by Eve Merriam, and *Machines at Work,* by Byron Barton.

Look for pendulums in the school environment. Swings are an example.

Helpful Hint

Place the pendulum on a tray to contain the objects that are knocked down.

3.18 All Fall Down
Variable Weight Pendulum

Description
This activity builds on previous pendulum experimentation (activity 3.17). Children can explore the effect of changing the weight of the pendulum as they attempt to knock down small bottles filled with water. The pendulum is made by suspending a film canister from a 6-inch hook in a pegboard divider. Children can vary the weight of the pendulum by changing the film canisters, which are filled with materials of differing weights.

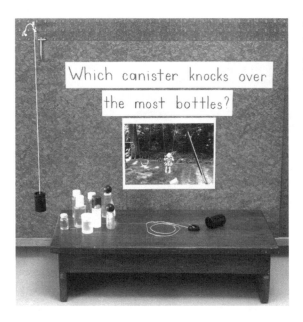

Child's Level
This activity is most appropriate for older preschool or kindergarten children who have had prior experience with pendulums.

Materials
▲ teacher-made pendulum, as described above
▲ small bottles filled with water and sealed
▲ film canisters with fillers of different weights (sand, cotton, pasta, and empty)

Scientific Information
The weight of the pendulum affects the force that can be exerted to knock down an object.

Sequence of Implementation
1. Start with two film canisters that differ markedly in weight.
2. Add additional canisters with a range of weights.
3. Take suggestions from the children for additional materials to add to the canisters.

What to Look For
Children may experiment to determine which canisters will knock down the bottles.
Children may try to knock down the bottles by attempting to throw the lightweight canisters rather than releasing them.
Some children may not yet realize where to place the bottles in order to knock them over.

Questions to Extend Thinking
How can you use the pendulum to knock down these bottles?
Do these canisters feel the same or different?
Do you think this canister will knock down the bottles?
Why did this canister knock down the bottles but this canister
    didn't?
Can you change the pendulum so it will knock down the bottles?

Modification
Add a score sheet or abacus so children can record how many
bottles they knocked down.

Integrated Curriculum Activities
Plan a math activity using the pendulum. Older children can see
    who can be the first to knock down ten bottles.
Encourage the children to make pendulum movements to music
    during group time.
Add a large pendulum to a gross-motor area (see activity 8.5).

Helpful Hint
Stores that develop film often have bins full of empty film canisters, which they are happy to give to teachers.

3.19 High, Low, Over They Go
Adjustable Pendulum

Description
The adjustable pendulum is an excellent follow-up to pendulum activities 3.17 and 3.18. In this activity, suspend the pendulum via connecting links so that the children can adjust the length of the pendulum and observe the effect. The pendulum is suspended from an infant gym.

"Topsy Turvy Trolls" pictured here by HearthSong.

Child's Level
This activity is most appropriate for older preschool or kindergarten children who have had experience with pendulums and can manipulate the length of the chain.

Materials
▲ pendulum made by using links to suspend a weight from an infant gym
▲ stacking clowns or other stackable objects to knock down

Scientific Information
The path of a pendulum is an arc. The distance that the pendulum can travel depends on the length of the rope or chain holding the weight.

Sequence of Implementation
1. Start with adjustable links for the chain and two stacking objects to knock down.
2. Add additional stacking objects as the children begin to experiment with shortening the chain.
3. Provide other hooks for suspending the chain that are off-center so children can experiment with this phenomenon.

What to Look For

Children will try to knock over the stacking objects with the pendulum.

As children shorten the chain on the pendulum, they may not understand why the pendulum misses the objects they are trying to knock down. They have to construct this relationship.

Some children may not yet realize where to place the stacking objects in order to hit them with the pendulum.

Children will experiment with lengthening and shortening the chain and moving the stacking objects.

Questions to Extend Thinking

How can you knock over all these clowns?

What happens when you make the chain shorter?

If I make the chain this short, how many clowns will I have to stack in order to knock any down?

How long do I have to make the chain in order to hit a clown this far away?

Modification

Add an observation journal to the area so that children can record the results of their experimentation.

Integrated Curriculum Activities

Use the adjustable pendulum for a painting activity (see activity 5.11) and allow the children to adjust the chain length as they paint.

Suspend a tire from a large A-frame so that children can swing on it and experience the feeling of being on a pendulum.

Helpful Hint

The pendulum frames used in activities 3.17 and 3.18 can also be used for this activity.

Science in the Sensory Table

Dawn had been busy pouring water onto a water wheel and watching it spin for some time. Sometimes she poured a lot of water and it spun fast. Other times she poured the water a little at a time and the wheel moved slowly. When one of the children who had been using the water table left, Dawn picked up his water wheel and stacked it on top of her own. She watched carefully as she poured water onto the top water wheel. "Look!" Dawn exclaimed. "When I pour water on this wheel, they both go around."

▲ ▲ ▲

Linda called to her teacher and asked for a bucket to catch the water that was flowing out of the water table. The teacher looked into the table to see what was causing the problem. Linda had constructed an elaborate array of pipes and fittings that connected the pipes at many angles. She was eagerly pouring water through the pipes and watching where it came out. Linda had not yet figured out how to keep the water inside the table when working with such an elaborate system of plumbing. Her solution was to place a bucket on the floor to catch the falling water. The teacher supplied the bucket. Linda was obviously learning a great deal about the movement of water, and the bucket was an important cog in the experimental process.

▲ ▲ ▲

The sensory table invites children to explore potentially messy materials with their hands. They respond eagerly to the opportunity to interact with materials that are often off limits. Children may spend hours watching how water fills and overflows a bottle or how sand turns the wheels of interlocking gears. As children endlessly explore and experiment, they make note of the results and construct important scientific relationships.

Teachers' Questions

Why is it important to include sensory table activities in the science curriculum?

Sensory table activities encourage the construction of physical knowledge with regard to both liquid and dry materials. The sensory table provides an ideal area for active experimentation since it is designed to contain a substantial volume of either liquid or dry substances. Children can experiment with how these materials react when used with simple machines, which can also be incorporated into the sensory table. For example, a funnel is a type of inclined plane, while an eggbeater employs a wheel and axle. Children can also explore the movement and containment of liquid and dry materials, buoyancy, absorption, and measurement through carefully planned sensory table activities.

What sensory table activities encourage the scientific process?

Most sensory table activities invite children to experiment and thereby encourage some construction of scientific knowledge, as long as the sensory table is not so cluttered that children cannot observe the results of their actions. However, specific activities are especially valuable for highlighting certain aspects of the scientific process:

▲ *Hypothesize*—Using clear tubing and corks with water encourages children to hypothesize about how they can stop or regulate the flow of water.

▲ *Observe*—Jars with holes in various places motivate children to observe carefully why water comes out of the jar at certain places and stops coming out once the water level is below the hole.

▲ *Predict*—Hooking pipes together challenges children to predict where either wet or dry materials will emerge.

▲ *Compare and Classify*—Using a sieve to strain cornmeal, rice, and beans stimulates children to compare the size of the individual materials to the holes in the tool they are using and classify the substances based on the results.

▲ *Infer*—Repeated experimentation leads children to form inferences. Something as simple as filling and refilling a bottle with water helps children realize that water moves upward as it is added to a contained area and then flows downward as it overflows the container.

▲ **Measure**—Different sizes of spoons or containers used in conjunction with either wet or dry materials encourage children to measure and explore volume.

▲ **Communicate**—Leading questions stimulate children to communicate the results of their explorations with many materials.

▲ **Create Relationships**—Combining physical action with specific materials or objects, such as pouring sand through a wheel or set of gears, helps children formulate relationships based on the physical characteristics of materials and how they can be affected.

What scientific principles emerge as children experiment with materials in the sensory table?

Children discover that the specific properties of liquid and dry materials may differ. For example, liquids flow while dry materials do not, and certain materials absorb liquids while others do not. Children also learn that buoyancy is a property of liquids, but not of dry materials. They can bury a cork under sand, but the cork always pops to the top of water.

Scientific principles are often related to specific activities. They are clarified in each activity in this chapter.

What is the teacher's role?

The teacher can encourage the construction of knowledge and the use of the scientific process through carefully planned activities and well-timed questions that stimulate thinking. The teacher must nurture a classroom atmosphere that is conducive to children's experimenting and trying things out. In addition, teachers should be equally excited by children's ideas or hypotheses that turn out to be incorrect as those that are right. Both lead to knowledge and are part of the scientific process.

What should teachers consider when planning sensory table activities?

Teachers should incorporate both short-term and long-range objectives in their planning. Utilizing seasonal materials, such as nuts in the fall or potting soil in the spring, reflects typical short-term considerations. Short-term planning might also relate to children's interests. Washing baby dolls with a variety of materials that differ in their absorption abilities might be incorporated if a child has a new baby at home. Long-range planning ensures that children have the opportunity to explore many scientific principles in the sensory area over time. Using simple machines or tools with both liquid and dry materials is an example of long-range planning.

As with other areas of the curriculum, teachers should also build upon the children's previous experiences in their planning. For example, teachers might follow a water activity with a similar activity using dry materials.

Whenever possible or appropriate, teachers should integrate sensory table activities with the overall curriculum. For instance, if the curriculum is centered around a construction theme, then pipes and fittings might be added to the water table.

What questions can teachers ask to stimulate thinking?

Teachers can ask questions that encourage children to explore and experiment or that focus on aspects of the scientific process (specific questions are included with each activity). For example:

▲ *Hypothesize or Predict*—Where do you think the water will go if you lift this end of the tube?

▲ *Compare or Classify Results*—Which materials are left in your strainer? Which fell through?

▲ *Infer and Create Relationships*—How can you use the sand to make the wheel move slowly?

▲ *Communicate Results*—What happened when you stirred the water and liquid soap with the whisk?

What criteria should teachers follow when designing a sensory area for the classroom?

Teachers should design the area to minimize management issues so that children can focus on the scientific possibilities of the area. Teachers must first decide how many children at a time can use the sensory table. Three or four is typical, although the size of the table has an obvious bearing on this. If only one child can use the area at a time, opportunities for communication and cooperative learning are minimized.

The sensory table should contain enough materials so that children can focus on scientific explorations rather than arguing about use of the materials. Ideally, there should be enough implements for each child at the table. For example, a sensory table designed for four children might contain four funnels, four buckets, and four cups for pouring. Teachers can make the sensory table self-limiting by including just enough smocks for the number of children who can use the table at a time. A waiting list allows children to sign up for a turn and know that they won't be missed.

The sensory table should be located away from quiet areas of the classroom, such as the writing table or the book area. Children often become excited as they explore sensory materials and the volume level may rise. Place protective covering under the sensory table if it is located in a carpeted area. Throw rugs can absorb water if the area becomes slippery. If teachers do not have a sensory table, plastic wash tubs can be used as a substitute for many of the activities.

What sensory materials can teachers include in the sensory table?

Teachers can alternate water with a wide variety of dry materials.

WET	DRY
water	rice
colored water	dried beans, peas, or corn
water with liquid soap	cornmeal
snow	sand
	nuts
	soil
	wood shavings
	combinations, such as cornmeal and rice
	paper confetti
	pea gravel

What implements can children use with sensory materials?

Children can use many tools or objects that encourage the movement, containment, or measurement of materials. They can also combine simple machines with sensory materials. The following implements are often incorporated into sensory table activities (see the activities in this chapter for additional ideas):

▲ funnels of various sizes and shapes
▲ clear plastic jars or bottles
▲ pumps
▲ marbles or small balls
▲ basters
▲ colanders, sieves, or slotted spoons
▲ eggbeaters and whisks

- ▲ ice cube trays
- ▲ freezable ice balls and other assorted shapes
- ▲ clear plastic tubing and corks
- ▲ water or sand wheels
- ▲ tongs
- ▲ measuring cups or spoons
- ▲ assorted sponges or cloth

Where can teachers find materials for the sensory table?

Parents are an excellent source of materials for the sensory area. A wish list posted on the door or sent home in a newsletter is often effective. Teachers can also find inexpensive materials for the sensory table in odd-lot or dollar stores, hardware stores, or kitchen supply stores. Natural materials can be collected for free.

How long should activities remain in the sensory table?

The sensory table should be available every day, if possible, and activities should be left out for at least a week to give children adequate time to explore them. The water must be changed every night to meet health regulations in many areas. Teachers may wish to follow a water activity with a similar activity involving dry materials.

How can teachers assess children's construction of scientific knowledge through use of the sensory table?

Teachers can carefully observe children as they interact with the materials and communicate with one another. Teachers can also ask pertinent questions to delve into children's thinking. Teachers may choose to record the information anecdotally or use an assessment tool, such as the one in appendix A.7. Suggestions for questions to ask and what to look for as children interact with sensory materials are included with each activity.

Sensory Table
Activities

4.1 Funnel Fun
Movement of Water

Description
Funnels are an adaptation of an inclined plane. Children can experiment with the way a funnel channels water from the wide end at the top of the funnel into a narrow opening in a bottle.

Child's Level
This activity is appropriate for either preschool or kindergarten children.

Materials
- ▲ funnels
- ▲ clear plastic bottles
- ▲ cups, for pouring the water
- ▲ water (colored with food coloring, if desired)

Scientific Information
Water flows down an inclined plane. A funnel bends the incline into a cone shape to channel water from a wide opening to a narrow opening.

Sequence of Implementation
1. Start with larger funnels, which may be easier for young children to manipulate.
2. Add a variety of sizes of funnels so children can experience the difference this makes as they pour the water into them.
3. Include some objects that won't move through the funnels, such as ice balls or corks.

What to Look For
Many children may try to fill the bottles without using the funnels, especially at first.

Children will experiment with using the funnels to fill the bottles and with watching the water run out of the bottom of the funnels.

Children may also try to pour water into the narrow end of the funnel.

Questions to Extend Thinking
What can you do with these funnels?
What happens to the water when you pour it into the funnel?
How can you use the funnel to help you fill the bottle?

Modification
After the children have experienced funnels with water, try using the same materials with a dry substance, such as sand.

Integrated Curriculum Activity
Some marble tracks have a funnel piece. This allows children to experiment with funnels in the manipulative area.

Helpful Hint
Clear funnels can be made by cutting the ends off of one- and two-liter plastic bottles.

4.2 Funnel Board
Movement of Dry Materials

Description
Young children often find it difficult to hold a funnel and bottle and still observe where the material they are pouring is going. The funnel board holds the funnel so children can more easily observe this process. You can make a funnel board by drilling 1-inch holes in a ¾-inch-thick piece of wood that is several inches shorter than the length of the sensory table. Screw a piece of wood to each end of the funnel board to elevate it above the level of the sensory table.

Funnel board pictured here available from Holcombs.

Child's Level
This activity is appropriate for either preschool or kindergarten children.

Materials
▲ funnel board, as described above
▲ funnels
▲ clear plastic bottles
▲ sand
▲ cups, for pouring

Scientific Information
Funnels are a type of inclined plane bent into a cone shape. They channel a fine-grained substance, such as sand, from a wide opening to a narrow opening.

Sequence of Implementation
1. Start with larger funnels for immediate success.
2. Switch to smaller funnels, which may plug up with sand if children pour it too quickly.
3. Add some objects that won't move through the funnel, such as marbles.

What to Look For
Children will watch intently as the sand falls through the funnels
   suspended on the funnel board.
Children will use the supported funnels to fill bottles with sand.
Children will put their hands under the funnels to catch the sand
   as it falls.
Children will make hills of sand at the bottom of their funnels.
Some children will pour sand into the holes in the funnel board
   without using the funnels to see what happens.

Questions to Extend Thinking
What happens to the sand when you pour it into the funnel?
Why won't the sand go down the funnel any more? (This happens
   when the hill of sand at the bottom of the funnel reaches the
   funnel.)
What happens when you pour the sand really fast?

Modification
Repeat the activity with water instead of sand once children have
had ample time to experiment with the sand.

Integrated Curriculum Activities
Use funnels and funnel boards in outside sand areas.
Add a funnel piece to marble tracks in the manipulative area.

Helpful Hint
The funnel board and funnels may be too high for smaller children to easily reach. If so, add a hollow wooden block or stool for
them to stand on.

4.3 Sand Wheels
Movement of Dry Materials

Description
Children are always intrigued with sand or water wheels. Through experimenting, they learn that the movement of a liquid or fine-grained dry substance can be used to turn a wheel and produce circular motion.

"Water Sand Mill" pictured here by Plasto Bambola.

Child's Level
This activity is appropriate for either preschool or kindergarten children.

Materials
- ▲ sand, or other dry material
- ▲ sand wheels
- ▲ cups, for pouring
- ▲ small buckets or bowls

Scientific Information
Movement of liquid or fine-grained materials can provide the energy to turn a wheel. This is the principle behind many machines. The amount of water or granules hitting the wheel affects how fast it turns.

Sequence of Implementation
1. Start with just the sand wheels and cups so that children can focus on how the sand moves the wheel.
2. Add small buckets or bowls to catch the sand. This encourages children to observe where the sand emerges from the wheel.
3. Add some objects that won't move through the sand wheel, such as ice balls or marbles. Children can observe the effect on the wheels.

What to Look For

Children will pour the sand into the wheels to watch them spin.

Children will open and close the doors on the wheels to observe the effect.

Some children will vary the speed at which they pour the sand to observe the result.

Children will make piles of sand at the bottom of their wheels.

Some children may stack wheels to see what happens.

Questions to Extend Thinking

What is making the wheel turn?

Where does the sand go after it moves through the wheel?

How can you make the wheel turn slowly?

What happens if you pour a lot of sand all at once?

How can you stop the wheel?

Modification

Over a period of time, children can experiment with how many different materials react with the wheels. Try a variety of dry substances, such as rice, beans, and dried corn, as well as water.

Integrated Curriculum Activities

Put gears in the science or manipulative areas of the classroom (see activities 3.15 and 3.16).

Sing songs about wheels, such as "The Wheels on the Bus."

Add colored sand to the art area for sand collages.

Helpful Hint

Some sand inevitably ends up on the floor. Provide children with small brooms and dust pans so they can assist in the cleanup.

4.4 Water Gears
Gear Adaptation

Description
Water can provide the force to turn gears. If you can't find commercial water table gears, make your own by mounting gears from commercial manipulative materials onto wooden frames. Lay out the gears on the wood so that they interlock. Mark the center holes of the gears on the wood. Drill holes in the wood to hold small pieces of narrow dowel rod. Children can place the gears on the dowels to experiment in the water table. Add small footings of wood to the bottom of the frames so they will stand unsupported.

"Water Wheels" pictured here by Sunny Park.

Child's Level
This activity is most appropriate for older preschool or kindergarten children.

Materials
▲ moveable gears and frames, as described above
▲ water
▲ cups, for pouring

Scientific Information
Movement of water can provide the force to turn gears.

Sequence of Implementation
1. Start with gears and frames so children can observe the effect that moving water has on them.
2. Later, switch to other types of gears from the manipulative area. Older children can construct a variety of configurations with them and experiment with the results.

What to Look For
Children will pour the water through the gears and observe the result.
Children will move the gears to various positions to see the effect.
Some children will vary the speed at which they pour the water to see what happens.

Questions to Extend Thinking
How can you make the gears turn?
What will happen if I take this middle gear off the frame?
How can you make the gears turn slowly?
Which direction is this wheel turning?

Modification
Use dry materials to turn the gears. After the children have experienced the gears with water, switch to a dry substance, such as rice or cornmeal.

Integrated Curriculum Activities
Coordinate sensory table gears with gears in the science area (activities 3.15 and 3.16).
Put a collection of small gears in the manipulative area for sorting and classifying. Parents can help supply the gears from old clocks or machinery.

Helpful Hint
When making the water table gears, be sure the dowel is thin enough for the gears to spin freely. The wood may swell slightly when wet.

4.5 Tubing and Corks
Movement of Water

Description
Clear plastic tubing allows children to experiment with the movement of water. They can tilt and bend the tubes and observe what happens to the water. Corks that fit into the tubes enable children to start and stop the flow of water.

Child's Level
This activity is appropriate for either preschool or kindergarten children.

Materials
▲ clear plastic tubing, approximately ¾ to 1 inch wide and 12 to 18 inches long
▲ water (colored with food coloring, if desired)
▲ corks that fit the tubes
▲ cups, for pouring
▲ funnels
▲ clear plastic bottles
▲ black marbles

Scientific Information
Water flows downward, if possible. When both ends of a tube are elevated, the water moves to the lowest point of the tube and back up both sides evenly.

Sequence of Implementation
1. Start with just the water, cups, and clear tubing so that children can focus on the movement of the water.
2. Add corks so children can start and stop the flow of water.
3. Introduce funnels to use as a tool to direct water flow into the tubes.
4. Add clear plastic bottles into which the tubing will fit. Directing water through the tubing and into the bottle is another way to experiment with the movement of water.
5. Add black marbles so children can observe how they react in tubes with water. Be sure the marbles can move freely through the tubing and won't get stuck.

What to Look For

Children will pour water into the tubes and move the ends of the tubing up and down to make the water move.

Children will experiment with lowering one end of the tube to let the water run out.

Some children will notice that the water runs out of the tube when they hold it in the air but not when the end is under the water.

Questions to Extend Thinking

Where do you think the water will go if you pour it in your tube?

What happens to the water if you lift up both ends of the tube?

Can you make the water stop at this spot on the tube?

What happens to the water you pour into the tube when the other end is under the water?

Modification

After children have had many opportunities to experiment with the tubing and water, switch to a dry substance, such as cornmeal, so they can compare how it reacts with the water.

Integrated Curriculum Activities

Read books about construction and plumbing, such as *Hammers, Nails, Planks and Paint,* by Thomas Campbell Jackson.

Add tubing to marble tracks in the manipulative area.

Take a walk with the children and look for the natural flow of water.

Helpful Hint

Aquarium supply stores or hardware stores are good sources for tubing.

4.6 Plumbing Connections
Movement of Water

Description
In this activity, children can connect pipes to a variety of fittings and observe how water moves through them. You can utilize pipe building sets that you may have with your manipulative materials or purchase component parts from hardware or building supply stores.

Child's Level
This activity is most appropriate for older preschool or kindergarten children.

Materials
▲ PVC pipes and fittings
▲ water
▲ cups, for pouring

Scientific Information
Water flows downward through an open channel. If a channel is blocked, water moves back upward. Water that is moving slowly is more likely to divert to a side channel, as when water moving upward in the pipes diverts into side pipes.

Sequence of Implementation
1. Start with straight pieces of pipe and fittings that will close off an end of the pipe. This is the most similar to other experiences children may have had, such as with bottles and lids or tubing and corks (activity 4.5).
2. Add elbow fittings so children can observe how they alter the flow of the water.
3. Include a variety of fittings for experimentation.

What to Look For

Children will start and stop the flow of water through the pipes by using their hands, by adding fittings, and by tilting the pipes.

Younger or less experienced children may just pour the water through a pipe without connecting pipes together.

Children will observe how the pipes channel the water.

Children will explore where the water will flow when there is more than one possible direction.

Children may not accurately predict where the water will come out of the pipes. Some water may land on the floor!

Questions to Extend Thinking

How can you use these pipes with the water?

What can you use to make the water stop?

Which piece should I use to make the water come out over here?

Which hole in this piece do you think the water will come out of?

Is there any way to make the water move up instead of down?

Modification

Children can compare how dry materials such as rice behave in the pipes once they have had many experiences using the pipes with water.

Integrated Curriculum Activities

Add a construction area to dramatic play. Include pipes for building.

Read books about how buildings are made and plumbing installed. *Skyscraper Going Up,* by Vicki Cobb, and *Hammers, Nails, Planks and Paint,* by Thomas Campbell Jackson, are examples.

Helpful Hints

Use a saw to cut PVC pipe to various lengths.

Place throw rugs under the water table if the area becomes slippery.

4.7 Jars and Holes
Water Pressure

Description
Clear plastic jars with holes cut in a variety of places allow children to experiment with water pressure and the movement of water.

For additional descriptions of this type of activity, see Physical Knowledge in Preschool Education *by Constance Kamii and Rheta DeVries.*

Child's Level
This activity is appropriate for either preschool or kindergarten children.

Materials
▲ clear plastic jars with holes cut in a variety of places
▲ clear plastic jars without holes
▲ cups, for pouring
▲ water (colored with food coloring, if desired)

Scientific Information
Water will move out of any opening in a container that is below the water level. The higher the column of water is above an opening, the more forcefully the water will stream out.

Sequence of Implementation
1. Start with jars that have just one hole cut in them. Have the holes at different places in different jars. Include some jars with no holes for comparison.
2. Add jars with more than one hole, including holes directly opposite each other.
3. Let children decide where they want holes cut in some jars so they can experiment with the results.

What to Look For

Children will fill the jars with water and may initially be surprised when it comes out of the holes.

Children will plug the holes with their fingers to stop the water flow.

Some children will notice that the column of water shooting out of a hole changes its arc as the water level decreases in the jar.

Some children will be surprised when water stops coming out of a hole due to the drop in the water level.

Questions to Extend Thinking

What is happening to the water?

Why won't the water come out of this hole any more?

Which hole do you think the water will come out of?

How can I get the water to come out of this hole?

Modification

Once children have had many opportunities to use the jars with water, introduce the jars with dry materials and let the children compare the results. Some dry materials come out of the holes and others don't. None of the dry materials come out as forcefully as the water.

Integrated Curriculum Activities

Older children may wish to graph which materials come out of the holes in the jars and which don't.

Try playing a recording that includes moving water in the background.

Use jars with holes in the outside sand area.

Helpful Hint

Substitute paper or Styrofoam cups for plastic jars if you have trouble cutting the holes or need a quick replacement. These cups, however, are not durable and do not enable children to observe the water as easily as clear jars.

4.8 Colander Mixtures
Filtering

Description
Children can use colanders for separating dry mixtures into their component parts. The bowl shape of the colander makes it especially easy for young children to use since the contents are less likely to fly out when they shake a colander than a sand sifter.

Child's Level
This activity is appropriate for either preschool or kindergarten children.

Materials
- ▲ mixture of cornmeal and beans
- ▲ colanders
- ▲ slotted spoons

Scientific Information
A filter can separate a mixture of materials. Larger particles are not able to pass through the holes of the filter. In this activity, the colander acts as a filter.

Sequence of Implementation
1. Start with colanders and a mixture of cornmeal and beans. This allows children to focus on how the holes in the colander separate the cornmeal from the beans.
2. Add slotted spoons. They also filter out cornmeal from beans.
3. Add additional substances to the mixture. Rice, cracked corn, or dried peas are possibilities.

What to Look For
Children may initially use the colanders as mixing bowls.
Children will shake the colanders and notice that the beans do not fall through the holes but the cornmeal does.
Children will use the slotted spoons as scoops and notice that the cornmeal filters through the holes.
Some children may make piles of cornmeal.

Questions to Extend Thinking
Why does the cornmeal keep coming out?
Why won't the beans come out?
What did you do to get a pile of only cornmeal?

Modification
Children can use other tools to filter dry mixtures. Strainers, sieves, and sifters are possibilities.

Integrated Curriculum Activities
Add colanders and slotted spoons to the sand area outside.
Include colanders and slotted spoons in the dramatic play area.
Use colanders and slotted spoons for a cooking activity, such as draining canned fruit for fruit salad.

Helpful Hint
Some cornmeal usually ends up on the floor. Provide small brooms and dust pans so the children can help with the cleanup.

4.9 Sifters
Filtering

Description
In this activity, children can use sifters to separate flour from rice. This is an excellent follow-up to activity 4.8, in which children use colanders to filter dry materials. The sifter allows children to accomplish the same task by just moving their fingers. A spring mechanism turns a wheel, which pushes the materials through the sifter.

Child's Level
This activity is appropriate for either preschool or kindergarten children.

Materials
▲ flour and rice mixed together
▲ sifters

Scientific Information
A filter can separate a mixture of materials. Larger particles are not able to pass through the holes of the filter. In this activity, the sifter acts as a filter.

Sequence of Implementation
1. Begin with a mixture of flour and rice for children to sift.
2. Add additional substances to the mixture, such as cracked corn, so children can notice the effect.

What to Look For
Children will squeeze the sifters and notice that only the flour falls through.
At first, some children will use the sifter as a cup for pouring.
Children will make hills of flour.

Questions to Extend Thinking

What happens when you squeeze the handle on the sifter?
Why won't the rice come out?
How did you make the wheel turn inside the sifter?

Modification

Children can also use sieves or strainers as sifting tools.

Integrated Curriculum Activities

Put a bakery in the dramatic play area.
Use sifters as part of a baking activity.
Read books about baking, such as *The Doorbell Rang,* by Pat
    Hutchins, and *Pizza Party,* by Grace Maccarone.
Use sifters to sprinkle colored salt or sand onto art creations.

Helpful Hint

If too much flour gets in the air, add more rice to the mixture or
try cornmeal instead.

4.10 Basters and Balls
Water Pressure

Description
In this activity, children can use directed water to move balls.
They must first construct how to get water into the basters.

Child's Level
This activity is appropriate for older
preschool or kindergarten children.

Materials
▲ basters
▲ assorted balls (Ping-Pong, golf, tennis,
spongy, Koosh, etc.)
▲ water

Scientific Information
Moving water has force. A directed stream
of water can be used to move things. Water
will move into a space once the air has
been forced out (as in the basters).

Sequence of Implementation
1. Start with one-piece basters and one type of ball. At first, children will be busy trying to figure out how the basters work.
2. Add other types of balls for experimentation.
3. If possible, try a different type of baster. Several styles are
   available, and some allow children to remove the tube from
   the part they squeeze.

What to Look For
Children will need to experiment to get the basters to work.
Children will use the squirting water to move the balls.
Some children will try to squirt each other with the water until
   redirected to aim at the balls.

Questions to Extend Thinking

How can you use these basters to move the balls?
Is there a way to move the balls without touching them with the
    baster or your hand?
Where do you have to squirt the ball to make it move over here?
How can you move the ball a long distance?

Modification

Moving air also moves objects. After children have had many
experiences moving balls with water, let them try moving them
using the basters without water, or with air.

Integrated Curriculum Activities

Read *Yellow Ball,* by Molly Bang. The moving water moves a ball
    across the ocean.
Play target games with balls in the gross-motor areas.
Put bellows and wind wheels in the science area.

Helpful Hint

Children often need clear ground rules with this activity to aim at
the balls and not each other.

4.11 Water Table Apothecary
Water Pressure

Description
Children are fascinated with using pipettes or eyedroppers to fill small bottles with colored water. They will engage in this activity seemingly endlessly!

Child's Level
This activity is most appropriate for older preschool or kindergarten children who can manipulate the eyedroppers.

Materials
▲ pipettes or eyedroppers
▲ an array of small bottles
▲ colored water

Scientific Information
Water will move into an area once the air has been forced out. Squeezing the top of the eyedropper or pipette forces the water out the narrow opening at the bottom.

Sequence of Implementation
1. Start with pipettes if they are available since they are easier for young children to manipulate than eyedroppers.
2. Switch to eyedroppers after the children have become somewhat adept at using the pipettes. You can start with eyedroppers if you can't obtain pipettes.

What to Look For
Children will need to experiment and practice in order to work the pipettes or eyedroppers.

Many children will be fascinated with filling the bottles and watching them overflow.

Some children will observe what proportion of a bottle they can fill with one pipette full of water.

Many children will pretend play with the bottles.

Questions to Extend Thinking
How can you use these pipettes to fill the bottles?
How can I make the water fill up my eyedropper?
How can you get just one drop of water to come out?
How many eyedroppers full of water does it take to fill this
     bottle?

Modification
At a later time, try adding basters and jars with lids for children
to fill. The basters operate on the same principle but hold a much
larger volume of water.

Integrated Curriculum Activities
Use eyedroppers or pipettes with colored water for an art activity.
This activity coordinates well with a doctor theme, since medicine
     is sometimes dispensed with eyedroppers. Try setting up a doc-
     tor or veterinary office in the dramatic play area.

Helpful Hints
You can often obtain pipettes from labs.
Parents who travel can supply an endless array of small bottles
     from hotels.

4.12 Tongs
Double Lever

Description
This activity gives children the opportunity to experiment with the movements and coordination necessary to lift objects with tongs. Children are eager to fill ice cube trays with objects. This encourages coordinated use of the tongs as they attempt to find objects buried in sand and place them in specific holes.

Child's Level
This activity is most appropriate for older preschool and kindergarten children.

Materials
- ▲ tongs
- ▲ objects to pick up with the tongs
- ▲ ice cube trays
- ▲ sand

Scientific Information
Tongs are a double lever, with each arm of the tong acting as a lever. The fulcrum is at the point where the two arms connect. Soft or rough objects are easier to grab with the tongs than hard, smooth objects.

Sequence of Implementation
1. Start with soft objects that are easier for children to lift. Pom-poms, small sponge balls, and cloth strawberries are possibilities. Use ice tongs at first since they are the simplest to use.
2. Switch to harder or smoother objects, such as nuts.
3. Introduce a variety of tongs. Egg tongs, salad tongs, and tea infuser tongs are all different.

What to Look For

Children will need practice and experience before they can operate the tongs.

Many children will be fascinated with lifting objects with the
tongs and moving them to compartments in the ice cube trays.

Some children will hide objects in the sand and try to find them
with the tongs.

Questions to Extend Thinking

How can you use these tongs to pick up the objects?

Which nut is harder to pick up, the rough one or the smooth one?

How many more nuts do you need to fill your tray?

Modification

Once children have become somewhat adept at using tongs with
objects in the sand, switch to ice balls and water. Floating objects
present a new challenge!

Integrated Curriculum Activity

Incorporate tongs with a math game, such as rolling a die and
picking up cloth strawberries with tongs. See *More Than
Counting*, by Sally Moomaw and Brenda Hieronymus, activity 2.1.

Helpful Hint

Check kitchen supply stores for various types of tongs. Tongs for
removing the stems from strawberries are short and chubby and
easy for children to use.

4.13 Net Fishing
Buoyancy

Description
Children can explore the buoyancy of various objects in water as they fish for them with small nets.

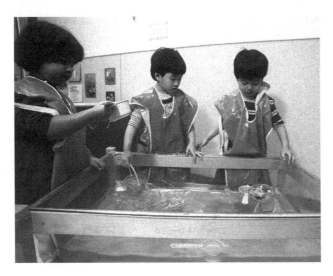

Child's Level
This activity is appropriate for either preschool or kindergarten children.

Materials
- ▲ strainers with handles and fish nets
- ▲ objects with varying buoyancy, such as ice balls, corks, large marbles, and sponge balls
- ▲ small buckets
- ▲ water

Scientific Information
When objects are the same size (volume), the one that is heavier is less likely to float. The heavier a sinking object is, the more quickly it sinks. The lighter a floating object is, the more of the object that stays above the water line.

Sequence of Implementation
1. Start with strainers, which are a little easier for children to handle than fish nets, and two objects that differ markedly as to buoyancy, such as ice balls and marbles.
2. Add additional objects with varying degrees of buoyancy, such as corks, spongy balls, shells, and small rocks.
3. Switch to fish nets, which are more of a challenge. Add plastic fish for fun.

What to Look For

Children will use the nets to fish for objects to collect in their buckets.

Children will notice that some objects always float, some objects always sink, and some objects float sometimes and sink sometimes.

Children will experiment with buoyancy by pushing down objects that float and releasing them and by attempting to get objects that normally sink to float.

Some children will figure out how to make objects that usually sink, such as the flatter shells, float instead.

Questions to Extend Thinking

Is there any way to get this ice ball to stay under the water?

Why won't my marble float? It looks as big as this ice ball.

What happened to the sponge ball? It was floating before, and now it sank.

Modification

Try adding some objects that are very large but float, such as a piece of balsa wood, and some objects that are small but sink, such as pennies.

Integrated Curriculum Activities

Read *King Bidgood's in the Bathtub,* by Audrey Wood. The characters also fish with nets.

Plan a treasure hunt path game for the math area. See *More Than Counting,* by Sally Moomaw and Brenda Hieronymus, activity 5.20.

Helpful Hint

Avoid simplistic answers for why things sink or float, such as heavy things sink and light things float. These are not accurate. Instead, guide children to make their own observations.

4.14 Sink the Boat
Buoyancy

Description

Children can explore the effect of additional weight on buoyancy in this activity by adding marbles to small plastic boats until the boats can no longer float. As a more unusual tool for catching the marbles, children use ladles. The unique vertical attachment of the ladle's handle requires a different movement to manipulate than children are accustomed to and presents an added challenge.

Child's Level

This activity is most appropriate for older preschool and kindergarten children.

Materials

▲ small plastic boats
▲ marbles
▲ ladles
▲ variety of small objects
▲ water

Scientific Information

As an object's weight increases while its volume remains the same, its ability to float decreases. Children will notice that as they add weight to a boat, more and more of the boat is under water until it finally sinks.

Sequence of Implementation

1. Start by putting marbles and boats in the water. As children add marbles to the boats, they can concentrate on the effect the marbles have on the buoyancy of the boats.
2. Add ladles as an added challenge for lifting the marbles.
3. Switch to a lightweight item, such as corks, so that children can compare the effect on the boats.
4. Add a variety of small objects of varying weights for exploration. Ice balls, pom-poms, gravel, teddy bear counters, corks, and plastic people are possibilities.

What to Look For
Children will add marbles to the boats and try to sink them.
Some children will quantify the number of marbles it takes to
sink a boat.
Some children will pretend play with the boats.
Children will initially find the ladles awkward as they try to
manipulate them like a spoon.
Children will compare how various objects affect the buoyancy of
the boats.

Comments and Questions to Extend Thinking
What do you think will happen to the boat if we add some
marbles to it?
If I add one more marble, do you think the boat will still float?
I wonder why that boat full of corks is still floating.
How can you use these ladles to catch the marbles?

Modification
Children can use other types of utensils for catching the marbles.
Slotted spoons are interesting because they allow the water to
escape while still holding the marbles.

Integrated Curriculum Activities
Read the predictable book *Who Sank the Boat?* by Pamela Allen.
Set up a beach in the dramatic play area. Fill a small wading pool
with sand and add sunglasses, beach towels, and an ice cream
stand.
Use sail boat stickers to make a grid math game. See *More Than
Counting,* by Sally Moomaw and Brenda Hieronymus,
chapter 4.

Helpful Hint
If you do not have small boats, use small microwave dishes, such
as those from baked potatoes.

4.15 Soak It Up
Absorption

Description
Children learn about how well materials absorb water by interacting tactilely with them. In this activity, children fill jars by soaking up water with a variety of materials and squeezing the water into the containers.

Child's Level
This activity is appropriate for either preschool or kindergarten children.

Materials
▲ clear plastic jars or buckets
▲ a variety of materials to soak in the water, such as terry cloth, vinyl, silk, net, fur, and sponge
▲ water

Scientific Information
Some materials absorb liquids better than others.

Sequence of Implementation
1. Start with buckets or jars and terry cloth wash rags so children can experience immediate success.
2. Add a second material that does not absorb water as well, such as vinyl.
3. Introduce additional materials for experimentation.

What to Look For
Children will soak up water with the cloths and squeeze it into the containers.
Children will make comparisons about how well the various materials soak up the water.
Some children may use the cloths to wash the water table.

Questions to Extend Thinking
How can you use this cloth to get the water into the bucket?
Which material has more water come out when you squeeze it?
What happens to the water on the vinyl?

Modification
After children have experimented with the cloths, they may want to use them to wash baby dolls. This extends interest in the activity.

Integrated Curriculum Activities
This sensory activity coordinates well with a quilt unit, where children are handling a variety of fabrics.
Put fabric samples in the art area for collages.
Read books about fabrics and quilts, such as *The Patchwork Quilt,* by Valorie Flourney, and *Charlie Needs a Cloak,* by Tomie de Paola.
Sing rain songs and talk about how clothes feel when they are wet.
Use eyedroppers to drip colored water onto coffee filters. Children can watch the paper absorb the water.

Helpful Hint
Ask parents from other cultures or international community organizations for donations of fabric samples from their cultures.

4.16 Dry It Out
Clothesline Pulley

Description
This activity combines clothes washing with a practical use of the pulley. A large wooden frame holds a clothesline pulley above the water table. As the children wash doll clothes, they can clip them to the clothesline and move them across the table.

Pulley frame pictured here available from Center Concepts Incorporated, 2414 Ashland Avenue, Cincinnati, Ohio 45206.

Child's Level
This activity is most appropriate for older preschool or kindergarten children.

Materials
- ▲ pulley frame
- ▲ doll clothes
- ▲ water and liquid soap
- ▲ clothespins
- ▲ scrub boards (optional)

Scientific Information
The pulley enables us to move objects without having to move ourselves. Material left hanging in the air dries out as the water evaporates. However, since this happens over time and children cannot see the process, they are not yet able to understand the cause and effect.

Sequence of Implementation
1. Start with doll clothes to wash so children can focus on the changes the soap and water make in the fabric.
2. Introduce scrub boards for rubbing, if available.
3. Add the clothesline pulley so children can observe how water drips from the wet clothes. This will also provide a more practical experience with the pulley.

What to Look For

Children will scrub the clothes to produce soapsuds.

Children will hang the clothes and watch the drips.

Children will use the pulley to move the clothesline and create additional space for hanging clothes.

Some children will be surprised when they pull the rope in one direction and the clothes move in another direction.

Some children may be surprised to come back later and find the clothes dry.

Questions to Extend Thinking

What should we do with these doll clothes and water?

How can we make the water soapy?

What happens to the water when you hang the clothes on the line?

How can you move the clothes in this direction?

Modification

If possible, occasionally hang wet clothes outside so children can observe how the wind affects the drying process.

Integrated Curriculum Activities

Set up a laundry in the dramatic play area. Include a washing machine, clothesline, and ironing board.

Read *A Pocket for Corduroy,* by Don Freeman, and *The Big Enough Helper,* by Nancy Hall. Both take place in Laundromats.

Helpful Hint

If clip clothespins are too difficult for some children to use, try starting with the push kind.

4.17 Eggbeaters and Whisks
Bubbles

Description
Children can use both eggbeaters and whisks to transform liquid soap and water into soapsuds. The eggbeater uses a wheel and axle for a crank. Both the eggbeater and whisk are adaptations of the lever bent into a curved shape.

Child's Level
This activity is appropriate for either preschool or kindergarten children.

Materials
- ▲ water
- ▲ liquid soap
- ▲ eggbeaters
- ▲ whisks

Scientific Information
Rapid movement transforms liquid soap and water into soapsuds. The eggbeater and whisk can be used as tools for moving water quickly. The wheel and axle on the eggbeater makes it easier to turn the blades more quickly than by finger movements alone.

Sequence of Implementation
1. Start with eggbeaters. Children like turning the cranks and are excited when soapsuds emerge.
2. Switch to whisks. They allow children to more easily feel the movement of the blades, which transfers into the movement of water.

What to Look For

Children will crank the eggbeaters and stir with the whisks to produce soapsuds.

Children will make as many soapsuds as possible!

Children are intrigued by feeling the soapsuds and sculpting them.

Children may observe the transformation of soap and water into soapsuds and back to milky water again.

Questions to Extend Thinking

What can you do with the eggbeaters?

What happened when you stirred the water with the whisks?

Can you explain to Susan how to make the soapsuds? She wants bubbles too.

Where did all the bubbles go that were here before?

Modification

After a few days, try adding food coloring to the water so children can compare how the water and bubbles look.

Integrated Curriculum Activities

For a resource with many bubble activities, see *Bubble Festival* (GEMS, Lawrence Hall of Science, University of California, Berkeley).

Make large bubble blowers by taping two soup cans together.

Read books about bubbles, such as *Bubble Bubble,* by Mercer Mayer.

Helpful Hint

Some liquid soaps make much better bubbles than others. Experiment with brands in your area or check with other teachers.

4.18 Scrubbing Fossils
Geology

Description
Scrubbing fossils and rocks with water and small brushes encourages children to examine them more carefully. The water makes details in the rocks more noticeable than when they are dry.

Child's Level
This activity is appropriate for either preschool or kindergarten children.

Materials
▲ fossils or rocks
▲ small brushes
▲ water

Scientific Information
Water brings out highlights in the color and configuration of rocks that are not as evident when they are dry.

Sequence of Implementation
1. Start with several rocks with imbedded fossils, if available. Otherwise, use rocks with interesting color patterns or configurations.
2. Add individual fossils or other types of rocks.

What to Look For
Children will examine the rocks more closely as they scrub them with water.
Children may notice that some of the fossils look like shells they may have seen.
Some fossils may break loose from the rock they are imbedded in as the children scrub them.

Questions to Extend Thinking
What can you see in this wet rock?
Are the lines easier to see in the wet rock or the dry rock?

Modification

Children can explore shells in the same manner. This is particularly interesting when they have been examining fossilized shells. Children can make comparisons between the shells and the fossils.

Integrated Curriculum Activities

Read books about fossils and geologists, such as *Digging Up Dinosaurs*, by Aliki, and *Bones, Bones, Dinosaur Bones*, by Byron Barton.

Examine fossils or minerals in the science area with magnifying glasses (activity 2.12).

Put a museum in the dramatic play area. Include fossils or rocks in the displays.

Helpful Hint

Ask children to contribute rocks for this activity. Get parents' permission for children to bring the collections to school.

Science in Art

*Michael used glue for the first time when he entered preschool.
He ignored the pieces of paper set out for the collage activity, but
he spent ten minutes painting the glue on the paper. Later, when
he retrieved his paper from the drying rack, he exclaimed with
distress, "My picture disappeared!" This was the first of many
scientific observations he would make about the changes in
materials.*

▲ ▲ ▲

*Detha explored the colored chalk by drawing with the point as
well as with the flat side. When she was satisfied, she used a
small spray bottle to mist her chalk drawing with water. When
she was dissatisfied with the results, she added more chalk and
more water until she felt her drawing was complete. Detha
explored both the movement of objects (physics) and changes in
materials (chemistry).*

▲ ▲ ▲

Can you remember the excitement you felt when you first
used watercolor paints and discovered that you could combine
two colors to create a new one? Perhaps you accidentally spilled
water on your paper and were amazed when it became a muted
wonder. Art experiences are a natural setting for many scientific
observations and provide a wealth of opportunities for children to
explore science through an integrated curriculum approach. Most
science books for young children focus on experiments or magical activities, so the classroom teacher is responsible for creating
more appropriate learning opportunities for children in the area
of science.

Art materials are intrinsically motivating to children and are a
part of most cultures. The organization of the art curriculum and
the questions the teacher asks create a myriad of opportunities
for children to explore and observe fluidity, the ability to adhere,

and transparency. They may also create relationships, such as same, different, light, and dark.

Teachers' Questions

What art activities promote the scientific process?

Art activities that focus on the process of exploration rather than the final product are the best activities to promote the scientific process. Two types of activities—those that involve the movement of objects and those that involve changes in materials—emphasize the scientific processes of observation, inference, and comparison of cause and effect relationships.

What types of art activities involve the movement of objects?

Painting activities provide opportunities for children to explore the movement of objects. The process of using a paintbrush in itself is a movement of an object. Other materials may also be used to apply paint. For example, painting with marbles (activity 5.7) encourages children to apply the paint to the paper by rolling it on an incline created by the slope of a shoe box. Children may hypothesize that the paint track will follow the movement of the marble and verify the hypothesis through observations. Children may also create relationships, such as more or less light or dark, as the marbles roll across the paper.

What art activities involve changes in materials?

Traditional experiences with glue and paint encourage children to closely observe the changes in materials, both those that occur immediately and those that occur over time. The activities in this book give teachers the information necessary to ask children questions that focus their attention on the scientific principles that emerge through their natural explorations of a creative media.

Why is it important to include art activities that incorporate the scientific process?

Early childhood educators recognize the importance of an integrated curriculum. The inclusion of scientific principles in the art area provides opportunities for children to create relationships among the other curricular areas. The child who glues sunflower seeds may also be interested in comparing a variety of seeds displayed in the science area (activity 2.9). Likewise the child who explores the inclines in the gross-motor areas (activity 8.1) may be motivated to further examine the physical properties of the incline by painting with marbles (activity 5.7).

What scientific principles emerge in the art area?

Art materials allow children to explore the properties of a variety of materials and observe changes in materials over time or in combination with other materials. Art activities further children's cognitive development as they present situations in which a variety of problems must be solved, such as how to attach nuts to paper and keep them from rolling off or what colors to combine to produce a third color. Teacher-designed art activities are an integrated part of the curriculum and progress from simple to complex. Teacher-designed art activities also provide a conducive atmosphere for the exploration of scientific principles, such as heavy objects require more glue to adhere them to a surface or that the force of gravity moves paint to the lowest point on the paper.

Do science activity books include science in the art area, and do art activity books promote science?

Science activity books rarely focus on art activities. Art activity books may focus on the end product rather than the process. However, even process-oriented art books do not give teachers information about the science imbedded in the individual activities and the ways to encourage children in pursuit of scientific information.

What art materials are needed to encourage scientific thinking?

Traditional art materials, such as paint, paper, glue, crayons, and chalk (used individually or in combination with unique implements) create opportunities for children to use the scientific processes in naturally occurring art activities. For example, the teacher may introduce chalk in three separate instances. First, the children explore colored chalk on paper. At a later date, the teacher may wet the paper before the children use the chalk for drawing. As an additional experience, the children draw with chalk on dry paper and then use a small spray bottle to wet the paper as desired. The children observe the results of adding water to a substance and may infer that water will alter the appearance of other substances as well. Continued explorations with art materials will confirm or deny that hypothesis, which is part of the scientific process.

Where can teachers find the unique materials needed to incorporate more science into the art curriculum?

Many of the supplies can be found in art supply catalogs, hardware stores, kitchen supply stores, odd-lot stores, and craft stores. Parents may also be able to supply some of the materials, and teachers will find more suggestions in the activity section of this chapter.

How do teachers plan specific activities?

Teachers should consider the needs and interests of the group when planning art activities. They may also consider ways to integrate a thematic topic into the art curriculum. For example, if children have been exploring shells in the science area (activity 2.13), teachers might have them use shells to create imprints in playdough or clay as a special art activity. Thoughtful planning of individual activities and the subsequent variations enable children to more easily construct knowledge about the physical properties of materials.

How do teachers sequence the activities for maximum learning potential?

Teachers may begin with a simple format and increase the complexity with each subsequent presentation of the activity. Teachers may also vary the implement children use, such as the size or type of painting tool, so that children can explore the same activity with a slight variation. Careful sequencing of the presentation encourages children to build on the physical knowledge constructed during previous explorations of the materials.

How long should each activity be available for children?

Typically, teachers plan for the easel to be available each day. A daily special art activity may also be planned as one of the classroom choices for children. The activities in this chapter may be planned either for the easel or as a special art activity. Each activity and the variations may be repeated several times during the school year. It is important to remember that children do not become bored with the repetition, but rather increase their mastery of the media and the understanding of the scientific principles within the activity. Other art materials remain on shelves in the art center for two to three weeks. Children select these materials as they might select activities in a manipulative area, the block area, writing table, or other activity centers in the classroom.

What is the teacher's role?

Teachers plan, organize, and set up the activities, ask well-timed questions, observe, plan extensions and subsequent variations, as well as assess children's understanding of scientific principles. The teacher observes children's interactions with the art materials and waits for an opportunity to make comments about the process. In some instances the teacher may ask a question to encourage a child to think about the physical properties of the materials or to consider the possibility of relationships among various materials or actions and reactions.

Why should teachers avoid complimenting children's art work?

It is imperative for teachers to avoid judgmental comments such as nice, good, and pretty. Such comments, though well intended, stifle the creative process both in terms of art and science. Children may direct their activities to producing products that adults admire rather than exploring the many possibilities inherent in materials. Instead, teachers can make comments and ask questions sparingly to encourage exploration and creativity. They need not expect a response to every comment or question.

How can teachers promote a better understanding of the scientific principles embedded in the art activities?

Teachers make comments and ask questions that focus children's attention on the observation of the physical properties of the materials, the movement of objects and materials, and the relationships that emerge as children use the art media. It is crucial that teachers allow children time to explore art materials for an extended period of time and without interruption.

How can teachers assess the children's understanding of the scientific process and scientific principles?

Teachers can record anecdotal records or use an observation-based check list form. An example of this type of observation tool is included in appendix A.8.

Art
Activities

5.1 Paintbrush Potpourri
Painting with Varieties of Brushes

Description
Brushes are the most common easel-painting implement in the art curriculum. The potential for scientific learning is found in children's movement of the paint and their observations of how the paint reacts when used with different brushes. Children also notice changes in the paint from wet to dry.

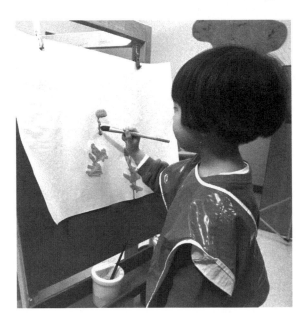

Child's Level
Painting with brushes is appropriate for preschool and kindergarten children.

Materials
- ▲ ¾-inch easel brushes
- ▲ chubby brushes
- ▲ watercolor brushes
- ▲ pastry brushes
- ▲ travel size makeup brushes
- ▲ paint, paint cups, and paper

Scientific Information
The physical properties of the brush affect the amount of paint it holds. The width of the bristles affects the width of the paint stroke on paper. The intensity of the color of the paint diminishes as the brush moves over the paper. The movement of the paint is a direct result of the movement of the child's arm. The brush is a lever.

Sequence of Implementation
1. Start with the standard easel brush. Children require extended periods of exploration with this type of brush. The younger or the less experienced the child, the greater the length of exploration time needed.
2. Switch to the chubby brush.
3. Include both the easel and chubby brushes.
4. Continue to introduce different types of brushes one at a time and compare them to other brushes. Eventually you can present several types of brushes in the same activity.

What to Look For

Children paint for the joy of painting, without regard for the type or width of the paint stroke created.

Some children notice the differences in the types of marks made.

Some children create patterns or use a specific brush for a specific purpose.

Some children will notice the effects of gravity as the paint drips down paper at the easel.

Comments and Questions to Extend Thinking

You've made a very thick (thin, long, wide) line of paint.

Which brush will you use to make a thinner line?

What would you do if you wanted to make a thinner (wider, darker) line?

Modifications

Use any of the brushes on the flat surface of a table so that children can observe the reactions of paint on a horizontal versus a vertical plane.

Vary the type of paint used with each of the brushes. You can add soap flakes, sand, sawdust, or other substances to alter the way the paint is moved by the brush.

Integrated Curriculum Activity

Use paintbrushes and water outside on the sidewalk or walls.

Helpful Hint

Unusual brushes can be found in kitchen supply stores.

5.2 Double Trouble
Painting with Double Brushes

Description
Painting with double brushes at the easel affords children an opportunity to apply paint with a familiar tool that reacts differently than expected. Children expect a paintbrush to be an extension of the painter's hand. The double brush requires children to consider the movement of paint in relationship to the design of the tool. Make the brushes by drilling holes into a block of wood and gluing the brushes into the holes.

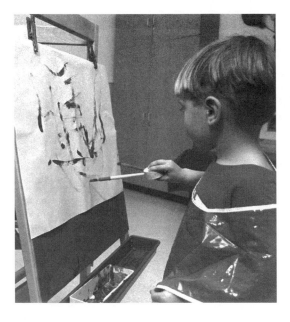

Inspiration for the brushes came from the design for Crazy Brushes in Constructive Play: Applying Piaget in the Preschool, *by George Forman and Fleet Hill.*

Child's Level
This painting tool is appropriate for older preschool and kindergarten children. Children need many experiences with regular brushes before the introduction of double brushes.

Materials
▲ inexpensive brushes with plastic handles
▲ pieces of wood (1 by 2 by 4 inches) or cylindrical slices of wood (1½ inch in diameter)
▲ quick-bonding glue
▲ paint, paint cups, and paper

Scientific Information
The movement of the paint is affected by the movement of the child's hand but is not a direct extension of the hand. The unusual positions of the double brushes directs where the paint goes. The brushes are a form of lever.

Sequence of Implementation
1. This is a very complex activity and should follow an extended exploration of brushes.
2. When you switch to the double brushes, continue using familiar paper and the paint.

What to Look For

Children ignore one of the brushes and paint as usual with a
single brush.

Children will solve the problem of getting paint on each of the
brushes. Some will put paint on one brush at a time; others
will position two paint cups so that they can dip each brush
into a separate cup at the same time.

Questions to Extend Thinking

How will you get paint on the brushes?

What did you do to make just one mark with the paintbrushes?

What would you do to put paint on both brushes at the same
time?

Modifications

Change the type of brushes attached to the handle.

Change the distance between the brushes on the handle.

Integrated Curriculum Activity

Use the double brushes with water on the sidewalk outside.

Helpful Hints

Ask a local hardware store or lumber yard for assistance finding
the right piece of wood for the handle.

Cylindrical slices of wood can be purchased at building supply
stores.

5.3 Roller Tracks
Painting with Rollers and Brayers

Description
Rollers and brayers (a tool for linoleum prints) can be used at the easel or on the table as tools for applying paint. This method is different from applying paint with brushes. Children move the paint by pushing a tool rather than stroking, as with a brush.

Child's Level
This activity is appropriate for preschool and kindergarten children.

Materials
- ▲ 3-inch-wide sponge rollers
- ▲ 2-inch-wide paint rollers
- ▲ 4-inch-wide brayers
- ▲ paint, small tray for the paint, and paper

Scientific Information
Sponge rollers and brayers absorb paint differently due to differences in their surfaces. They make tracks that differ from one another and also from brush marks.

Sequence of Implementation
1. Begin with the sponge roller.
2. Introduce the brayer for contrast.
3. Provide both the sponge roller and brayer in one activity so that children can compare the two.
4. Compare the sponge roller or the brayer to a brush in the same activity.

What to Look For

Some children may attempt to use the sponge roller as a brush.
Some children may not want to use the sponge roller or brayer.
Some children may notice the different type of paint tracks made
   by the sponge roller and brayer.

Questions to Extend Thinking

How can you make a wider (darker, bigger) paint track?
What would you do to make a lighter (darker, wider) paint track?

Modifications

Use a smaller size sponge roller for comparison.
Compare painting with a sponge roller to painting with a pizza
   cutter.

Integrated Curriculum Activities

Plan a construction site in the dramatic play area and include
   paint rollers.
Attach a section of butcher paper to a wall for a class painting
   project.

Helpful Hint

Trays from microwave entrees are an inexpensive source for trays
to hold the paint.

5.4 Nature's Paintbrushes
Painting with Natural Materials

Description
Many natural materials can be used as painting tools at the easel. The best tools are the ones that respond similarly to brushes.

Child's Level
This activity is most appropriate for older preschool and kindergarten children.

Materials
▲ evergreen branches, weeds, feathers, feather dusters, twigs
▲ small tray for holding the paint
▲ paint and paper

Scientific Information
The movement of the paint is affected by the movement of the child's hand. The paint track is a result of the size, shape, and type of painting tool used.

Sequence of Implementation
1. Introduce one type of natural item at a time.
2. Compare two or more types of natural items in the same activity.
3. Compare easel brushes to one or more natural items in the same activity.

What to Look For
Some children may not know how to paint with the unfamiliar items.
Some children may make comparisons among natural items.

Questions to Extend Thinking
How can you move the paint from here to here?
What happens when you make several strokes before you add
    more paint?
What type of mark does the feather make?
Can you tell which line you made with the stick?

Modifications
Use any of the natural materials alone or in combination on a flat
    surface, such as a table or the floor.
As a group activity, paint with any of the items on a large piece of
    butcher paper attached to a wall.

Integrated Curriculum Activities
Place the book *Owl Babies,* by Martin Waddel, in the reading
    area. The owl nest is described as filled with branches from the
    tree. Plan to paint with a branch.
Place the book *Feathers for Lunch,* by Lois Ehlert, in the reading
    area when planning the painting with feathers activity.
Take a nature walk to gather items for painting.

Helpful Hint
Provide small amounts of paint in the trays. Adding a large
amount of paint to any painting implement will only decrease the
unique patterns it creates.

5.5 Sponge Prints
Painting with Pliable Materials

Description
Printing is a form of painting in which the paint is applied by pressing a printing tool onto the paper. In other forms of painting, such as with brushes and rollers, the paint is applied by a fluid movement of the arm.

Child's Level
This activity is appropriate for preschool and kindergarten children.

Materials
- ▲ sponge brushes, available at hardware stores
- ▲ sponges cut into shapes, such as hearts, flowers, or apples
- ▲ natural sponges
- ▲ a small tray for paint
- ▲ paint and paper

Scientific Information
A sponge holds paint on its surface and in its small holes. The print impression on the paper is directly related to the size, shape, and texture of the sponge. The paint impression becomes lighter with repeated printings until more paint is added to the sponge.

Sequence of Implementation
1. Begin with the sponge brushes. They are the most similar to easel brushes and allow children opportunities to make connections to previous experiences.
2. Introduce shaped sponges.
3. Introduce natural sponges for comparison.

What to Look For

Many children will use the sponge brush like an easel brush and
make strokes of paint on the paper instead of printing.

Some children will create a relationship between the sponge and
the print made on the paper.

Older, more experienced children may create patterns.

Many children will be surprised when the sponges stick to the
paper.

Comments and Questions to Extend Thinking

I notice that this print is lighter (darker) than this one.

How can you make a print of the sponge?

What happens if you "hop" the sponge on the paper?

What would you do to make a darker (lighter) print?

Modifications

Plan an activity that uses two sizes of sponges on handles.

Use the same sponges for printing on a horizontal surface, such
as a table.

Divide easel paper or other paper into 4-inch grids to encourage
printing one impression into each square (one-to-one corre-
spondence). This may also encourage printing versus painting
with the sponge.

Integrated Curriculum Activities

When using sponges shaped like fruits and vegetables, plan a produce market in the dramatic play area.

Include the book *Swimmy,* by Leo Lionni, when using the natural
sponges.

Use sponges in the water table.

Helpful Hint

Cut your own sponge shapes from expandable sponges, available
in kitchen supply stores. You can create fairly intricate designs
before you add water to expand the sponges.

5.6 Cookie Cutter Prints
Painting with Rigid Materials

Description
Printing with cookie cutters and other implements is similar to printing with sponges. The major difference lies in the relationship created between the implement and the impression on the paper. The print made by cookie cutters and other rigid implements is exactly the shape and size of the implement. Children have less control over the outcome of the print since these tools typically make only one design each. A sponge can be turned in various positions for printing and thus produce various designs.

Child's Level
This activity is appropriate for preschool and kindergarten children.

Materials
- ▲ a variety of cookie cutters
- ▲ potato mashers in several styles
- ▲ lids from various types of jars or bottles, such as detergent, deodorant, and milk
- ▲ spools in assorted sizes
- ▲ small tray for the paint
- ▲ paint and paper

Scientific Information
The printing implement holds a fixed amount of paint that is transferred onto the paper. The print impression becomes fainter with successive prints until more paint is added. The impression made on the paper depends on the size and shape of the implement that is used.

Sequence of Implementation
1. Introduce one type of cookie cutter or other printing implement.
2. Change to a different printing implement.
3. Compare two or more printing implements in one activity.

What to Look For
Some children will attempt to use the cookie cutter like a brush by sweeping it across the paper.
Some children will repeat the printing process on the paper or create patterns.

Comments and Questions to Extend Thinking
How can you make a darker (lighter) print?
Look how the print matches the shape of the potato masher.
I notice that the print you made looks just like the shape of the cookie cutter.

Modifications
Compare a cookie cutter and sponge of the same shape.
Compare cookie cutters in the same shape, but different sizes.
Compare two different types of potato mashers.
Compare a selection of several different circle shapes, such as spools, film canisters, and detergent bottle lids.
Mark the easel paper into 4-inch squares to encourage children to print rather than paint with the implement, and make one print in each square.
Use any of the implements on a horizontal surface, such as a table.

Integrated Curriculum Activities
Use printing implements with playdough (activity 5.22).
Use potato mashers in a cooking activity.

Helpful Hint
Use plastic rather than metal cookie cutters. The metal ones bend when children press them onto paper.

5.7 Marble Marvels
Painting with Marbles and Balls

Description
Painting with marbles is an extension of the ramp activities children may experience in other areas of the curriculum, such as those found in chapter 3 (Machines and Pendulums), and chapter 8 (Science in Gross-Motor Areas). In this activity children further explore the properties of ramps in a medium that produces a permanent record of marble tracks on paper. This may help children create relationships between the actions and reactions of objects on a ramp.

Child's Level
Both preschool and kindergarten children will benefit from painting with marbles after some experiences with ramps, such as those in activities 3.1 and 8.1.

Materials
▲ plastic or cardboard box
▲ paper cut to fit the inside dimension of the box
▲ enough marbles for each child to have one marble
▲ small containers for paint
▲ tasting spoons for lifting the marbles out of the paint
▲ paint and paper

Scientific Information
The movement of the marble is caused by changing the slope of the box. Children can vary the angle and slope of the box and thus vary the reaction of the marble. The movement of the marble and resulting paint track is immediate and observable to the child.

Sequence of Implementation
1. Begin with one marble and one color of paint for each child. Children can fully explore the properties of the ramp, the marble, and the paint, as well as the effects of moving the ramp.
2. Use two or more marbles and two or more colors of paint.
3. Use a contrasting ball, such as a tennis ball, and one color of paint.

4. Use the marble and the tennis ball at the same time for comparison.
5. Use other combinations of marbles and balls with one or more colors of paint.

What to Look For

Many children will initially shake the box up and down to watch the marbles jump.

Some children will rapidly move the box back and forth without attending to the reactions of the objects inside.

Some children will slowly move the box back and forth to observe the track made by the paint on the objects.

Experienced children may attempt to control the movement of the marble to create a specific track or design.

Experienced children may predict which object will make a larger or smaller track.

Questions to Extend Thinking

How can you make the marbles roll in the box?

How can you make the paint track go from here to here?

What would you do to make the red and yellow tracks cross?

How can you make two tracks at the same time?

Modification

Try other types of balls, such as whiffle, golf, Ping-Pong, and Koosh.

Integrated Curriculum Activities

Roll objects down a ramp in the science area of the classroom (activity 3.1).

Plan ramp bowling or ski ball in the gross-motor areas (activities 8.1 and 8.2).

Create a ramp for tricycles in the outdoor area.

Helpful Hint

A clear box with a clear lid will keep the marbles contained but observable.

5.8 Downhill Painting
Painting on Inclines

Description
This ramp painting activity is similar to painting with marbles (activity 5.7), but the result is very different. Children release a roller down a ramp. The roller has been modified with pieces of sponge attached to it and covered with paint. The child is challenged to create a relationship between the design on the roller and the paint design that results from rolling it down the ramp.

Child's Level
This activity is most appropriate for older preschool and kindergarten children.

Materials
- ▲ ramp, made from a hollow block or a piece of wood supported by a small box so that an incline is created
- ▲ paper cut to fit the length and width of the ramp
- ▲ roller, made from a cylindrical block or tube to which four or more sponge pieces have been glued
- ▲ paint and brush for applying the paint to the sponge pieces

Scientific Information
The slope of the ramp affects both the speed and direction of the roller. The steeper the ramp, the faster the roller moves down it.

Sequence of Implementation
1. Begin with a fixed ramp so that children focus on the effect of the design made on the paper.
2. Add a plain cylinder so that children can compare it to the cylinder with sponge pieces.
3. Switch to a movable ramp, such as the ramp used in activity 3.3, so that children can adjust the slope.

What to Look For

Some children may push the roller without letting go of it.

Some children will release the roller and observe the resulting track.

Some children will adjust the slope of the ramp to increase the speed of the roller.

Some children will predict what will happen before they release the roller.

Questions to Extend Thinking

How can you make the roller move down the ramp and make a paint track?

What would you do to make a paint track over here?

Is there a way to keep the roller from moving so fast?

What is making the design?

Modification

Use some of the marbles and balls from activity 5.7 to roll down the ramp.

Integrated Curriculum Activities

Plan to roll objects down a large ramp in the gross-motor areas (activity 8.1).

Include ramp activities in the science area (see activities 3.1 through 3.6).

Helpful Hint

Do not use water soluble glue to attach the sponge pieces to the cylinder.

5.9 Dribble Dribble
Painting with Pulleys

Description
This painting activity uses a pulley mechanism suspended above a large sheet of paper. A rope threaded between two pulleys is attached to the backs of the chairs. A paint container is suspended upside down from the rope. Children can observe what happens when paint dribbles out of the container as it is pulled across the paper.

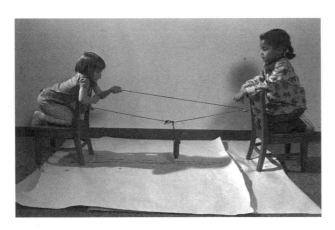

Child's Level
The pulley activity is appropriate for preschool and kindergarten children who have had experiences with pulleys.

Materials
- ▲ two small pulleys and appropriately sized rope, as shown
- ▲ a container for the paint that allows the paint to drip, such as one with an adjustable cap
- ▲ paint
- ▲ large sheets of paper

Scientific Information
A pulley allows children to move the paint container across the table while sitting or standing in one spot. The speed with which children pull the rope affects where the paint lands on the paper.

Sequence of Implementation
1. Begin with the paint container adjusted to release a slow stream of paint.
2. Allow children to regulate the flow of the paint by adjusting the opening of the paint container.
3. Try two containers of paint on the pulley system.

What to Look For

Many children will be more interested in the movement of the
pulley than in the process of applying paint to the paper.

Some children will pull on the rope and thus move the container
of paint.

Some children will attempt to control the movement of the paint
container in order to control the paint track.

Questions to Extend Thinking

How can you move the paint container across the paper without
touching it?

What would you do to make a steady stream of paint come out of
the container?

Where would you pull on the rope to move the paint container
over here?

Modification

Fill the container with powdered paint and apply it to wet paper.

Integrated Curriculum Activities

Plan to use a pulley system over the sand area and fill the container with water.

Set up a pulley system in the gross-motor areas (activity 8.3).

Experiment with pulleys in the science area (activities 3.13
and 3.14).

Helpful Hint

Hair-color application bottles with adjustable openings work well
for this activity. Be sure to poke a hole near the bottom of the
container or the paint will not come out.

5.10 Wheel Tracks
Painting with Wheels

Description
Wheels can be used as painting tools to provide a wide variety of possibilities. You can use traditional wheels found on toy vehicles, but you can also become creative and use casters from old furniture, pizza cutters, and pastry wheels.

Child's Level
Painting with wheels is appropriate for preschool and kindergarten children.

Materials
- ▲ small plastic vehicles, one for each child
- ▲ paper cut to fit the surface of the table
- ▲ a tray for the paint
- ▲ a variety of types of wheels, such as pizza wheels, pastry wheels, castors, and spools
- ▲ paint and large sheets of paper

Scientific Information
The movement of the paint is a result of the movement of the child's hand and the movement of the painting implement.

Sequence of Implementation
1. Provide one small vehicle for each child and one color of paint.
2. Compare the pizza wheel and the pastry wheel.
3. Introduce other types of wheels for painting implements.

What to Look For
Some children will enjoy moving the vehicles across the paper without regard for the paint track.

Some children will attempt to control the movement of the paint across the paper.

Some children will compare the tracks made by different implements.

Questions to Extend Thinking

What will you do to make more than one mark?
How can you move the paint from here to here?
What would you do to cover the paper with tracks?
How did you get two tracks when you only moved the car once?

Modification

Place fingerpaint on a tray and allow children to move the vehicles or other implements through the paint. Make a monoprint if desired.

Integrated Curriculum Activities

Use the small vehicles in wet sand to make tracks.
Plan to roll small vehicles down a ramp (activity 3.2).

Helpful Hint

Microwave entree containers are an inexpensive source for the trays.

5.11 Ellipses
Painting with Pendulums

Description
Using paint and the pendulum to create wonderful elliptical designs is an exciting classroom activity. The pendulum can be any size, but an infant gym, as shown, is a manageable size for the classroom. The design is a result of the properties of the pendulum and the way the child swings it.

Child's Level
This painting activity is appropriate for preschool and kindergarten children who have had experiences exploring the properties of the pendulum, as described in chapter 3, "Machines and Pendulums."

Materials
- ▲ an infant gym or similar structure, as shown
- ▲ a container with an adjustable opening
- ▲ large sheets of paper for the painting surface
- ▲ an old shower curtain to protect the area around the pendulum
- ▲ paint

Scientific Information
As the pendulum swings, an elliptical design is created. The longer the pendulum is allowed to continue its movement, the more the design will become apparent. Children may also create a straight line by swinging the pendulum back and forth.

Sequence of Implementation
1. Demonstrate the process for children after discussing their predictions of what will happen.
2. Ask children to release the container of paint and watch what happens.
3. Allow children to have more control over the opening of the paint container and the movement of the pendulum.

What to Look For

Children will be very excited and almost unable to refrain from
    stopping the pendulum each time it comes close to them.
Some children will notice the design the pendulum makes.
Some children will adjust the flow of paint in order to create a
    specific type of design.

Questions to Extend Thinking

What will happen if you don't stop the pendulum?
How can you make more paint come out of the hole?

Modification

Substitute colored sand for paint in the container and cover the
paper with media mix, liquid starch, or diluted white glue.

Integrated Curriculum Activities

Plan to include pendulum activities in the gross-motor areas
    (activities 8.5 and 8.6).
Design a pendulum activity for the science area (activities 3.17,
    3.18, and 3.19).
Set up a pendulum over the sand area. Fill the container with
    water so that children can observe the track it makes.

Helpful Hints

The pendulum paintings will require a large area and a long
    period of time for drying.
Poke a hole near the bottom of the paint container or the paint
    will not come out.

5.12 Misty Creations
Painting with Sprayers

Description
Small spray bottles can be filled with either diluted paint or colored water and then used to create interesting and muted color combinations. This activity works well at the easel, either inside or outside.

Child's Level
This activity is most appropriate for older preschool or kindergarten children.

Materials
▲ spray bottles that can be manipulated by small hands
▲ diluted paint or food coloring diluted with water
▲ large sheets of paper
▲ protective covering under the easel

Scientific Information
The spray bottle requires children to create a relationship between how hard they squeeze the handle and how much paint comes out. They may also construct a relationship between how fast the handle is pumped and how fast the liquid sprays. The effects of gravity are very apparent as the colors run down the paper. Changes occur in the paint when the colors mix together and when the paint dries.

Sequence of Implementation
1. Begin with large spray bottles, which are easier for children to work, and paint or colored water in two primary colors. Children can observe how these colors combine to form a third color.
2. Add the third primary color.
3. Switch to smaller spray bottles, such as hair misters.

What to Look For
Some children may experience difficulty operating the spray bottles.
Some children will soak the paper with the liquid.
Some children will become aware of the colors mixing and create intentional combinations.

Questions to Extend Thinking
Where do you squeeze the bottle to make the paint come out?
What would you do to mix these two colors?
How did you get orange? There's no orange paint in any of these bottles.

Modification
Use spray bottles filled with colored water to wet crayon drawings. Children will notice that the colored water does not adhere to the crayon.

Integrated Curriculum Activities
Plan to spray snow with food coloring (if you live in an area with snow).
Use the spray bottles to wet chalk paintings (activity 5.23).
Put pump soap dispenser bottles in the water table.
Use spray bottles filled with water as an outside activity.

Helpful Hint
Children may need to be redirected to spray only onto the paper.

5.13 Squirt and Blow
Effects of Air

Description
In this activity, children use bulb syringes or straws to move paint across paper. These devices further children's knowledge of the effects of air and the properties of paint. This easily assembled activity is best planned for a horizontal plane, such as a table or the floor. It would be too difficult for children to focus on the movement of the paint while contending with the effects of gravity at the easel.

Child's Level
This activity requires some ability to squeeze a bulb syringe or blow through a straw. You can observe the abilities of preschool children and determine the appropriateness of this activity. Most kindergarten children will have little or no difficulty with either the bulb syringe or blowing through a straw.

Materials
- ▲ bulb syringes or 6-inch sections of plastic straws (one straw for each child)
- ▲ watercolor paint or tempera paint, thinned with water
- ▲ tasting spoons or pipettes for applying the paint to the paper
- ▲ paper

Scientific Information
Air squeezed from the bulb syringe or blown through the straw causes the movement of the paint across the paper. The force of the air determines the resulting movement of the paint. More force causes more movement than a small amount of force. Mixing two or more colors of paint creates a change in color.

Sequence of Implementation
1. Straws are more familiar implements than bulb syringes and may be best as a first experience moving paint.
2. Start with one color of very thin paint. This affords children time to construct the skill necessary to blow enough air through the straw before focusing on mixing the paint.
3. Add one or more colors of paint.
4. Repeat the sequence using the bulb syringe.

What to Look For
Some children will be unable to figure out how to aim the air so that the paint moves.

Some children will attempt to move the paint by using the straw or syringe as a brush.

Some children will become aware of how they moved the paint and gain more control over the process so they can create intentional results.

Comments and Questions to Extend Thinking
How can you move the paint using the straw (syringe)?

Watch how Rosetta blows through the straw. (Use this statement to help a child figure out how to be successful by observing another child.)

What would you do to move the paint over to this side of the paper?

How can you mix these colors together?

Modification
Use eye droppers, which are similar to the syringes, to drop the paint onto the paper before blowing the paint.

Integrated Curriculum Activities
Use bulb syringes in the sensory table (activity 4.10).

Blow bubbles in jars with straws and soapy water.

Helpful Hint
Cut a small hole in the straws to prevent children from sucking up paint.

5.14 Spin-It Art
Painting with Revolving Surfaces

Description
Exploring the movement of paint becomes quite a challenge when the paper is in motion, as in this activity. You can substitute a turntable or a lazy Susan tray for the more traditional carnival spin-art activity. Children must consider not only the motion of their own bodies but also the continuous motion of the paper. They have control over the speed of the turntable or lazy Susan tray and therefore the outcome of the painting or drawing process. Since this activity may seem somewhat magical, this control by the child is very important in the construction of cause and effect relationships.

Child's Level
This activity is appropriate for older preschool and kindergarten children. Younger children do not have the experiences with traditional painting and drawing activities that lay a foundation for understanding this more unusual one.

Materials
- ▲ turntable with a variable speed adjustment
- ▲ lazy Susan tray
- ▲ paper plates, or paper cut to fit the lazy Susan tray
- ▲ markers
- ▲ cotton swabs
- ▲ paint

Scientific Information
Holding a drawing or painting implement still over a revolving base produces a matching circular pattern on the paper.

Sequence of Implementation

1. Begin with the turntable set on the slowest speed. Place the paper plate on the spindle and offer a selection of markers for children to use. After a period of exploration, children very often change the speed of the turntable or ask for a new paper plate.
2. After one or two days of experimentation with markers, offer children cotton swabs and two colors of paint to use on the paper plate.
3. Switch to the lazy Susan. This gives children more control over the movement of the paper.

What to Look For

At first children may attempt to move the marker along with the rotating plate. Therefore, no marks appear on the plate.

Children will figure out that they can hold the marker still and the spinning plate will cause the marker to draw circles.

Some children will experiment with various movements of the marker to create concentric circles or other designs on the plate.

Younger children may be fascinated by piling the markers on top of the plate and watching them spin off. They may even increase the speed of the turntable to make them spin off faster.

Questions to Extend Thinking

What happens if you don't move the marker?

Where do you place the marker to make a small (large) circle?

What would you do to make two circles at the same time?

Modification

Let children drip colored water or diluted paint from an eyedropper onto the rotating paper and observe the results.

Integrated Curriculum Activities

Include a Sit-n-Spin in the gross-motor areas.

Have children lie across a tire swing suspended over a large sheet of butcher paper. Spin the swing as they hold a marker over the paper to create a design (activity 8.6).

Helpful Hint

Secure the needle arm of the turntable with tape so that is does not interfere in the activity.

5.15 Vary the Paper
Effects of Absorption

Description
The physical properties of paper include the color, texture, and quality of absorption. The outcome of any painting activity changes when the paper is different. The observations of these outcomes lead children to construct knowledge about absorption.

Child's Level
This activity is appropriate for preschool and kindergarten children.

Materials
- ▲ white construction paper
- ▲ paper towels
- ▲ coffee filters
- ▲ additional drawing surfaces, such as fingerpaint paper, aluminum foil, acetate, corrugated paper, cellophane, or cardboard
- ▲ various types of paint and painting implements

Scientific Information
The physical properties of the paper affect the amount of absorption.

Sequence of Implementation
1. Start with white construction paper, watercolor paint, and brushes.
2. Change to paper towels but use the same paint and brushes as in the first experience.
3. Switch to coffee filters. Continue using the same paint and brushes as in the first experience.
4. Introduce other types of paper. Fingerpaint paper and aluminum foil have different absorbent characteristics than corrugated paper or cardboard.
5. Try all of the papers over a period of time with a variety of paints and painting implements.

What to Look For
Most children will not become aware of the differences in the types of drawing surfaces until they have had repeated experiences with all of them.

Some children may be dissatisfied when the paint soaks into the paper towel or coffee filter.

Some children will experiment with the effects of the paint on different drawing surfaces and make comments about the results.

Comments and Questions to Extend Thinking
Look at what happened to the paint.

What happens when you hold your brush still on the paper?

Modification
Drop diluted paint or colored water onto the papers with eyedroppers and observe the results.

Integrated Curriculum Activity
Experiment with the absorption properties of other materials in the sensory table (activity 4.15).

Helpful Hint
Place thin sponge pieces, such as those found in gift boxes of fruit, under the paper towels and coffee filters to absorb the excess paint. This makes cleanup easier.

5.16 Gobs of Glue
Creating Collages

Description
Experimenting with glue and a variety of collage materials allows children to create relationships about the physical properties of glue relative to various collage materials and surfaces. Careful planning by the teacher will enhance the possibilities for children to construct this knowledge.

Child's Level
This activity is appropriate for preschool and kindergarten children.

Materials
▲ white glue, full strength or slightly diluted
▲ various types of collage materials, such as paper, tissue, cellophane, ribbon, pasta shells, cotton balls, bottle caps, beans, seeds, and weeds
▲ various types of gluing surfaces, such as paper, cardboard, and wood

Scientific Information
Wet glue is liquid, white, and sticky and cannot adhere objects to each other. Dry glue is solid, colorless, and not sticky; however, as glue dries it acquires adhesion capabilities. Heavier materials require more glue to adhere them together or to a surface. The thicker the application of glue, the longer the drying time required.

Sequence of Implementation
1. Begin with small pieces of paper to glue to larger pieces of paper. Children require time to explore the glue before they are ready to be challenged by heavy materials.
2. Offer other lightweight materials to glue to paper. Some possibilities include ribbon and wrapping paper.
3. Provide lightweight materials that are more challenging for children to manipulate. Possibilities include cotton balls, tissue, and cellophane. The properties of these materials add new possibilities to explore.
4. Plan other collage experiences with heavier materials to glue onto cardboard or wood.

What to Look For

Children may initially ignore the collage materials and spend an extended period of time exploring the glue. Many children at first believe that the glue is white paint and cover the paper with glue while ignoring the collage materials.

Many children will layer glue and paper, one on top of the other, to create several layers.

Some children will use too much or too little glue to hold the materials.

Some children will construct an accurate relationship between the type of material and the amount of glue needed for adhesion.

Comments and Questions to Extend Thinking

I notice that you decided not to use the ribbon on your picture.
Do you want to use these leaves with the glue?
Is there another way to make the pasta stick to the paper?
When you hang your picture, do you think the paper will stick?

Modification

Plan a glue activity at the easel. The challenge of dealing with the effects of gravity adds a new dimension to the activity.

Integrated Curriculum Activities

Plan to glue nature items that might also be part of a science display, such as nuts or seeds.
Use glue and collage materials for a group collage.

Helpful Hint

Use a flat surface for drying collages made with heavy materials, such as acorns or shells.

5.17 Melting Crayons
Effects of Heat

Description
Melting crayons on a warming tray is a science experience in which the children's observations are especially important. You are responsible for the safety issues and must control the amount of heat involved. Children control the movement of the crayon on the warm surface and determine how hard to press and how long to hold the crayon in one place.

Child's Level
This activity is most appropriate for older preschool or kindergarten children.

Materials
▲ old crayons, with wrappers removed
▲ electric warming tray
▲ child-sized work gloves
▲ aluminum foil, waxed paper, cellophane

Scientific Information
Heat changes the composition of crayons from a solid to a liquid form. The degree of heat and the pressure on the crayon affect the speed at which the crayons melt. The melted crayon returns to a solid form almost immediately when removed from the warming tray. The color of the crayon is not affected by the heat, but colors may mix to create new colors if they flow together while in a liquid state.

Sequence of Implementation
1. Begin with a selection of crayons and aluminum foil.
2. Change the surface to waxed paper, which responds a little differently than aluminum foil.
3. Switch the surface to cellophane. (Try this out on your tray first to be sure that the heat is not too high.)

What to Look For
Children often view this activity as magical until they have time
to observe the relationships between heat and crayons.
Children may want to melt the crayons completely by dropping
them on the tray.
Some children will blend two melted crayons together.
Children will notice that the melted crayons quickly return to a
solid form when they are removed from the tray.

Questions to Extend Thinking
What is happening to the crayon?
Is there a way to make the crayon melt faster?
What do you think will happen when we take the paper off the
tray?

Modification
Sprinkle glitter on the melted crayon before removing the paper
from the tray. As the crayon hardens, it holds the glitter.

Integrated Curriculum Activities
Allow children to break or grate old crayons into small pieces.
Place the pieces in muffin pans sprayed with a non-stick spray.
Place the pan in the oven after it warms to 250 degrees and is
then turned off. The result will be multicolor crayons in a disk
shape.
Explore melting in cooking activities, such as adding butter to
pancakes.
Freeze colored water to form ice cubes. Add the ice cubes to the
water table so children can observe them as they melt.

Helpful Hint
Ask parents for donations of old crayons.

5.18 Squeeze It
Exploring Playdough

Playdough Recipe
2 cups flour
2 cups water
1 cup salt
3 tablespoons cream of tartar
2 tablespoons oil

Mix all the ingredients together in a medium saucepan. Cook over a medium-high heat until the ingredients clump together. Cool the playdough and knead.

Description
Playdough is a common material in early childhood classrooms and homes. The activity will help children construct knowledge about the physical properties of dough and its reactions to their manipulations. They can quickly note how their actions change the dough.

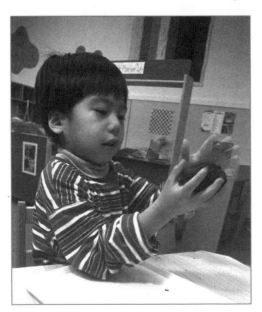

Child's Level
This activity is appropriate for preschool and kindergarten children.

Materials
- ▲ teacher-made playdough
- ▲ enough trays for each child at the activity table
- ▲ small rolling pins or short sections of 1-inch dowel rods

Scientific Information
Playdough can be squeezed, rolled, poked, and pushed. Manipulating the dough will change its shape. Playdough keeps its shape over time, or until it is manipulated by the child. Exposure to air dries the surface of the dough.

Sequence of Implementation

1. Start with playdough alone so that children can manipulate it with their fingers and experiment with the properties of the dough.
2. Add small rolling pins or short sections of 1-inch dowel rods. Children can experiment with their effect on the dough.
3. Try the playdough variations described in activities 5.19 and 5.20.

What to Look For

Some children will smell and try to taste the dough.

Many children have difficulty rolling the dough into balls. They need to experiment for a long time to figure this out.

Children need experience in order to discover how to flatten the dough with the rollers.

Comments and Questions to Extend Thinking

When you squeeze the dough, it pushes through your fingers.

What do you think will happen to the holes you made in the dough?

Is there a way to flatten the playdough?

Modifications

Add food coloring to water in the recipe.

Add scented oil in place of the cooking oil.

Include marbles with the dough for added interest.

Integrated Curriculum Activities

Plan cooking activities with dough, such as making pretzels and bread (activity 7.5).

Some children might want to make dough sculptures and allow them to dry completely.

Include *Earth Daughter,* by Joseph Ancona, in the reading area. Vivid photographs show an Acoma Pueblo girl working clay with her hands.

Helpful Hint

Store the playdough in an air-tight container to prevent it from drying out. It does not need to be refrigerated.

5.19 Can You Cut It?
Cutting Playdough

Description
Cutting playdough with a tool furthers children's knowledge of the properties of dough and the reactions of the dough to simple machines. This activity allows children to manipulate tools and compare how they affect the dough.

Child's Level
This activity is appropriate for preschool and kindergarten children.

Materials
▲ teacher-made playdough (see activity 5.18 for the recipe)
▲ scissors, plastic knives, spatulas, pastry and pizza wheels

Scientific Information
Playdough can be cut into pieces using a variety of tools. The work of cutting the dough is made easier by using a tool. The individual tools have similarities and differences.

Sequence of Implementation
1. Add scissors to the dough after children have had many experiences exploring it with their hands.
2. Change the cutting implement to the plastic knife.
3. Switch to a spatula. It responds similarly to the knife when cutting the dough.
4. Plan an activity that includes both a knife and a spatula so children can compare the two.
5. Introduce the pastry and pizza wheels so children can observe how two implements that look very similar also have differences.

What to Look For

Some children may ignore the tools and explore the dough with their hands.

Children will use the implements to cut the dough.

Some children may compare the similarities and differences among the cutting tools.

Children may become more skillful at cutting paper after experiences cutting the playdough with scissors.

Children will compare the differences in cuts made by the pizza and pastry wheels.

Questions to Extend Thinking

What can you do with these wheels?

How can you make smaller pieces of the dough?

What happens when you push the pizza wheel through the dough?

What did you use to make this zigzag line? (pastry wheel)

What did you use to make this straight line? (pizza wheel)

Modifications

Use craft sticks in place of the plastic knives for very young children.

Use the same tools with Silly Putty for very different results.

Integrated Curriculum Activities

Use knives to cut fruit for a cooking activity.

Use pastry and pizza wheels as painting tools (activity 5.10).

Helpful Hint

Save plastic knives from fast food restaurants.

5.20 Mash It, Smash It
Squeezing Playdough

Description
Squeezing playdough with tools is an extension of activity 5.18 in which children use their hands to squeeze the dough. The tools provide additional feedback about the physical properties of the dough and allow children to better understand simple machines.

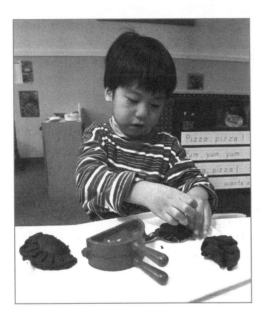

Child's Level
This activity is appropriate for both preschool and kindergarten children.

Materials
- ▲ teacher-made playdough (see activity 5.18 for the recipe)
- ▲ lemon squeezer
- ▲ dumpling maker

Scientific Information
The implements used to squeeze the dough are variations of the lever. Each tool is formed by two levers, which makes the work of squeezing easier than it would be with hands alone. The lemon squeezer and dumpling maker each compress the dough and make unique impressions.

Sequence of Implementation
1. Provide many opportunities for children to explore playdough by squeezing it with their hands.
2. Add the lemon squeezer for a different squeezing experience.
3. Introduce the dumpling maker after the lemon squeezer. It is more difficult to handle.
4. Plan to use the lemon squeezer and dumpling maker together for comparison. The design of each tool is similar but the effect on the dough is different.

What to Look For

Children may push the lemon squeezer into the dough like a
cookie cutter instead of squeezing the two sides of it together
with dough in the middle.

Children will explore the lemon squeezer and dumpling maker to
determine how much dough can be placed between the two
pieces.

Some children will compare the impressions made by the lemon
squeezer and the dumpling maker.

Questions to Extend Thinking

What can you do with this lemon squeezer?

How did you make that shape with the dough?

What will happen if you use a small piece of dough in the
squeezer?

Modification

Use other sizes of dumpling makers.

Integrated Curriculum Activities

Use the dumpling maker for a cooking activity.

Use the lemon squeezer to make lemonade.

Helpful Hint

Look for these tools in odd-lot and discount stores.

5.21 Squiggles
Pressing Playdough

Description
In this activity, children push playdough through a garlic press or sink strainer and thus change the dough from a whole into many small parts. Playdough can also be pushed through a meat grinder with similar results.

Child's Level
This activity is appropriate for older preschool and kindergarten children.

Materials
- ▲ teacher-made playdough (see activity 5.18 for the recipe)
- ▲ garlic press
- ▲ sink strainer
- ▲ small grinder

Scientific Information
Playdough can be changed in shape, separated into pieces, and then reformed into the original mass. The more dough that is pushed through a garlic press or a strainer, the longer the squiggles grow. The grinder is a combination wheel and axle and screw while the garlic press is a double lever with the fulcrum at the hinge. The work of separating the dough is made easier by the use of simple machines.

Sequence of Implementation
1. Begin with the garlic press. Children find it fascinating.
2. Introduce the sink strainer. The results are similar to the garlic press, but children have to push the dough through the holes.
3. Offer the sink strainer and garlic press together for comparison.
4. Introduce the meat grinder.

What to Look For

Some children will experiment for a long time before figuring out how to load the dough into the garlic press.

Children will be delighted to observe the long squiggles of dough emerge from the garlic press.

Children will construct how to add more dough to the press and make longer squiggles.

Some children will press the strainer into the dough to make an impression rather than pushing dough through the holes.

Children may cooperate when using the meat grinder. One child may load the dough into the chute while the other turns the crank.

Questions to Extend Thinking

How can you make longer squiggles of dough come out of the holes?

What happens if you push the dough through the strainer?

Is there another way to make dough come out of the holes?

Modification

Add scissors to the activity for children to cut the squiggles.

Integrated Curriculum Activities

Use the sink strainer as a sieve in the sensory table.

Make peanut butter with the meat grinder (activity 7.8).

Helpful Hint

Purchase inexpensive, one-piece garlic presses at discount stores.

5.22 Impressions
Imprinting Playdough

Description
Through using a variety of tools, toys, and nature items, children discover more about playdough. Pressing the objects into the dough makes an impression that matches the design of the object.

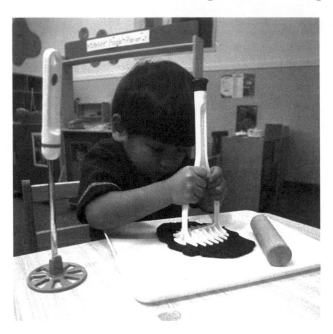

Child's Level
This activity is appropriate for either preschool or kindergarten children.

Materials
▲ teacher-made playdough (see activity 5.18 for the recipe)
▲ potato mashers, cookie cutters, shells, fossils, plastic gears, Bristle Blocks, or other interesting items

Scientific Information
Playdough can be molded or imprinted and retains that shape until handled again. The impression in the dough matches the design of the tool used to create the imprint.

Sequence of Implementation
1. Begin with cookie cutters since children may already be familiar with them as a printing tool with paint (activity 5.6).
2. Introduce other implements, one at a time, for exploration.

What to Look For
Some children may ignore the tools and use their hands to manipulate the dough.
Some children may recognize the relationship between the tool and the impression in the dough.
Some children may try to create designs with the tools.

Questions to Extend Thinking

What happens if you press harder with the potato masher?
Is there another way to press the gear into the dough?
What did you use to create this image?

Modifications

Include small rollers made from short sections of 1-inch wooden
  dowels.
Try some of the implements with Silly Putty for very different
  results.

Integrated Curriculum Activities

Use some of the implements as tools for a printing activity
  (activity 5.6).
Use the potato masher in a cooking activity.

Helpful Hint

Take suggestions from the children for other objects to use as
imprinting tools.

5.23 Muted Wonders
Drawing with Chalk

Description
This activity explores many possibilities for using chalk. Chalk is available in plain white, pastel, or bright colors, and a variety of sizes and shapes. You can create dozens of different experiences with chalk by changing the type of chalk, the type of paper, or by adding other materials.

Child's Level
This activity is appropriate for preschool and kindergarten children.

Materials
- ▲ various types of chalk
- ▲ construction paper or other drawing paper (not newsprint)
- ▲ small spray bottles filled with water

Scientific Information
When pressed on paper, chalk transfers its color onto the paper. The intensity of the color is a direct result of the pressure applied to the chalk. A powdery substance (chalk dust) is a by-product of drawing with the chalk. Chalk impressions can be partially erased from the paper. The addition of water to chalk drawings changes the appearance of the drawing. These are all physical properties of chalk.

Sequence of Implementation
1. Begin with white chalk on dark paper for high contrast.
2. Offer three or four pieces of colored chalk for each child.
3. Wet the paper before children begin to draw. This affects how the chalk transfers onto the paper.
4. During a future experience, allow children to wet the chalk drawings when they are finished. This alters the appearance of the chalk. Give each child a small spray bottle filled with water.

What to Look For

Children will use the chalk in the same ways they use crayons. They will draw with the point and with the side of the chalk.

Some children will experiment with different ways to hold the chalk to obtain different results.

Children will rub the chalk and notice that it smears.

Questions to Extend Thinking

What can you do to make a darker (lighter) mark with the chalk?

Is there another way to hold the chalk?

What happened when you added the water?

What did you do to create this wide line?

Modification

Cover the paper with buttermilk before drawing with chalk.

Integrated Curriculum Activities

Use chalk on the sidewalk.

Read the book *It Looked Like Spilt Milk,* by Charles G. Shaw, to coordinate with white chalk on dark blue paper.

Rub chalk over salt or sand to color it. Layer the salt in clear jars for a sand sculpture.

Helpful Hint

Break the long, thin pieces of chalk in half before giving them to children.

Science in Music

Samudra used a wooden mallet to gleefully pound on two clay flower pots that were suspended from a wooden frame in the music area of his classroom. He clearly enjoyed hearing the sounds he was making. Suddenly Samudra stopped his activity and looked intently at the two sizes of flower pots. He carefully struck the larger pot with his mallet; then he hit the smaller pot and listened closely. Samudra looked surprised and excited. Again and again he went back and forth between the two pots as he listened to the different pitches they each produced. Samudra had discovered that the size of the flower pots affected the tones they produced.

▲ ▲ ▲

Nancy played two different sizes of wood blocks in the music center and compared the sounds they produced. The small one had a much higher pitch than the larger one. After several minutes of striking the wood blocks with a wooden beater, Nancy experimented with pulling the stick end of the beater across the grooves on the larger wood block. This created a completely different sound. Nancy called to her friend Sylvia and showed her how to produce this new sound. Both girls experimented with the wood blocks as they sang a class song.

▲ ▲ ▲

Music and the science of sound are intertwined. As children explore and create music, they also construct relationships about the nature of sound and the factors that affect both sound and music. Children gain an awareness of how the physical properties of an instrument or object relate to the sound it produces and how their actions can also alter that sound.

Teachers' Questions

How is music related to science?

Acoustics is the science of sound. Understanding the properties of sound and the factors that affect it enables both children and adults to manipulate sound to create music and to express themselves. Children often begin by experimenting with sound-producing objects or instruments and noting the results. Their explorations lead to an increased understanding of how they can alter sounds or sequence sounds to create something new. Children's musical creations are frequently an outgrowth of their experimentation with the physics of sound.

What science concepts can children construct through music activities?

*Children construct concepts about **pitch** (how high or low a sound is), **dynamics** (how loud or soft a sound is), and **timbre** (tone quality).* They learn that the size of an instrument affects the pitch; large instruments have lower sounds than small instruments. Children also learn that the type of tool used to play an instrument affects the loudness of the sound that can be produced. A hard wooden mallet makes a louder sound on an instrument than a soft felt mallet even if the same force is applied. Through repeated experiences children recognize that the material an instrument is made from affects its sound. Wooden instruments sound different from metal ones, and instruments with strings have their own unique sound.

What types of music activities encourage the scientific process?

Music activities that encourage children to make comparisons, create relationships, and hypothesize promote the scientific process. Children must be able to physically interact with instruments or sound-producing materials in order to understand the relationship between objects and the sounds they produce. Therefore, music activities that allow children extended periods of time to explore instruments are ideal for promoting the scientific process. For example, children might play two sizes of triangles and compare the sounds they make. As they repeat this process with other instruments that are identical except for size differences, children can construct the relationship that the size of an instrument affects its pitch. When confronted with a new type of instrument, children might then hypothesize that the smaller instrument will have a higher sound.

How can teachers encourage children to explore the relationships between science and music?

Teachers can create a music area as a permanent part of their classrooms. This enables children extended periods of time to explore instruments and experiment with sound. Teachers can change the contents of the music area to focus on different scientific principles related to sound and music. For example, children might compare the sounds produced by three maracas with different fillers in order to explore timbre and dynamics. (Rice not only creates a different type of rattle than beans in a maraca but also has a softer sound.) At another time, children might compare maracas that are identical except for size. This encourages children to construct the relationship between size and pitch.

What should teachers consider when designing music areas for their classrooms?

Teachers should consider the location of the area, how large to make it, and what materials are needed.

Since a primary goal of the music area is to encourage children to explore the sounds they can produce on musical instruments, the expectation is that the area will be somewhat noisy. Therefore, it should be located away from quieter areas of the classroom, such as the writing center or book area.

Communication and the sharing of ideas constitute an important part of the scientific process. Therefore, the music area should be large enough to accommodate two to three children comfortably.

The music center should include a low bench or small table to hold several instruments and a divider or shelf to section off the area from the rest of the room and provide a space to hang related pictures and relevant print. Since some instruments need to be suspended, such as triangles or clay disks, a small wooden frame to hold them is an ideal addition to the music area. A frame can be easily made by screwing together four pieces of wood (each 4 inches wide by 20 inches long). Add two strips of wood to the bottom of the frame to keep it from tipping over. Attach hooks to the top of the frame for suspending the instruments. The specific contents of the area should be changed regularly so that children can explore many music activities and their relationship to science.

What is the teacher's role?

The teacher's primary role is to facilitate children's understanding of the relationship between science concepts and music.

Teachers can plan specific activities that encourage children to focus on these relationships. Many are included in this chapter. In addition, teachers can direct children's attention to particular aspects of sound through well-timed comments or questions.

What questions can teachers ask to stimulate thinking?

Teachers can ask questions that encourage children to draw relationships between the sounds or music they are creating and scientific principles. For example, if the teacher wants to direct attention to the relationship between size and pitch, she might ask, "If I want my tune to go up, which bar should I play next?" If the purpose of the activity is to explore dynamics, the teacher might ask, "Which beater would you use to make a quiet sound on the drum?" Ideas for specific questions are included with each activity in this chapter.

Where can teachers find music materials to promote the scientific process?

Teachers can design activities using instruments they already have to encourage the scientific exploration of sound in music. Many instruments can be easily made from inexpensive materials. See the activities in this chapter for ideas. Additional directions for making instruments can be found in *More Than Singing,* by Sally Moomaw.

How long should materials remain in the music area?

Children need repeated opportunities to return to instruments in order to construct physical knowledge related to sound. Therefore, each activity is usually left out for two or three weeks. Small changes or additions to the area may be made during this time, such as the addition of a third size of the same type of instrument or a different type of beater.

How can teachers assess the development of children's scientific knowledge in the music area?

Teachers can listen and observe as children create and explore in the music area. They can encourage children to communicate their observations to one another. This might be done through an observation sheet, area diary, or through dictations made to the teacher. Teachers can ask questions to delve into children's thinking and encourage communication. Teachers can record this information anecdotally or on an assessment sheet (see appendix A.9 for an example of this observation tool).

Music
Activities

6.1 Triangle Trio
Pitch

Description
The size of an instrument affects its pitch, or how high or low it sounds. This music center gives children the opportunity to explore the relationship between size and pitch. Three triangles, two identical in size and one smaller, are suspended from a wooden frame in the music area. Through experimenting with the triangles, children can discover that the two triangles that are the same size sound the same, but the triangle that is smaller has a higher pitch.

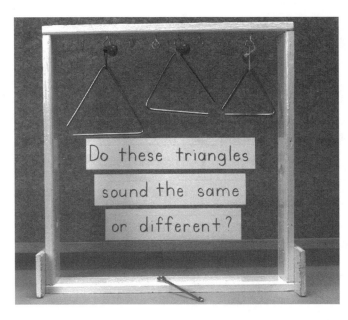

Child's Level
This activity is appropriate for either preschool or kindergarten children. For safety reasons, have very young children use spoons instead of metal strikers to play the triangles.

Materials
▲ three triangles, two the same size and one smaller
▲ wooden frame, or pegboard divider with hooks, to suspend the triangles

Scientific Information
Smaller instruments are higher in pitch than larger instruments. The smaller the instrument, the higher the number of vibrations per second.

Sequence of Implementation
1. If the children are not familiar with triangles, start with two identical triangles so that they can explore the physical properties of the instruments before focusing on pitch.
2. Introduce a triangle that differs in size from the first two so that children can experiment with how size affects pitch.
3. Add a third size of triangle if available.

What to Look For

Children will play the triangles and compare how they sound.

Some children will reverse the labels for high and low. You can model the appropriate labels when you take your turn playing the triangles.

Some children will hold the triangles with their hands, which deadens the tone. This is another discovery they can make.

Questions to Extend Thinking

How do the triangles sound?

Do all of the triangles look the same?

Do any of the triangles sound the same?

Why do you think this triangle sounds different?

Modification

Children can use the triangles at group time to accompany a song or rhythm activity. For ideas, see *More Than Singing,* by Sally Moomaw.

Integrated Curriculum Activities

Listen for triangles in recorded music. "Anitra's Dance" from Grieg's *Peer Gynt Suite* is a good example.

Children can interact with triangular shapes in the manipulative and art areas.

Helpful Hint

The triangles can be suspended with thick rubber bands or pipe cleaners. The holders that come with them always seem to fall off.

6.2 Can Band
Pitch

Description
Experimenting with the sounds of cans of many sizes allows children to explore the relationship between size and pitch. The smallest cans have the highest sounds and the largest cans have the lowest sounds. Children can discover that there is a whole range of pitch possibilities related to size.

Child's Level
This activity is appropriate for either preschool or kindergarten children.

Materials
- ▲ assortment of empty bi-metal cans, with the labels removed
- ▲ wooden beater, made from a macramé bead with a 7-inch wooden dowel glued into the hole

Scientific Information
The size of an instrument affects its pitch. The smaller the instrument, the higher the number of vibrations per second, and therefore the higher the pitch.

Sequence of Implementation
1. Start with several cans of varying size, but include two that are the same size for comparison purposes.
2. Add cans of additional sizes.

What to Look For

Children will play rhythms on the cans.

Children will notice that the cans have different sounds.

Some children will draw a relationship between the size of the can and its relative pitch.

Questions to Extend Thinking

Do these cans sound the same or different?

Which can do you think has the lowest sound?

Can you find any cans that sound the same?

Why do you think this can sounds so high?

Modification

Try introducing a can that is unopened but has the label removed. It looks like the other cans but sounds very different. The full can sounds "thunky" in comparison with the hollow cans. Many instruments are hollow to increase their resonance.

Integrated Curriculum Activities

Read books about children experimenting with found materials for instruments. *Max Found Two Sticks,* by Brian Pinkney, and *Max, the Music-Maker,* by Miriam B. Strecher and Alice S. Kandell, are examples.

Include vegetable and fruit cans in the dramatic play area.

Helpful Hint

Check the edges of the cans to be sure they are not sharp.

6.3 Glissando Cans
Timbre, Pitch

Description
The glissando cans present an unusual timbre for children to explore. They are made from metal cans that are partially filled with water and sealed shut. The cans are suspended from a wooden frame and struck with a wooden beater. As the water in the cans moves, it causes the pitch to slide up and down, called a *glissando*. The varying sizes of the cans also affects their relative pitch, with the smaller cans having higher glissandos than the larger ones. Paint or wax cans work well for this activity because their lids can be easily resealed.

Child's Level
This activity is most appropriate for older preschool and kindergarten children.

Materials
- ▲ empty metal wax, varnish, or paint cans of various sizes, with a small amount of water added before they are resealed
- ▲ wooden frame to hold the suspended cans
- ▲ wooden beater, made from a macramé bead with a 7-inch wooden dowel glued into the hole
- ▲ spray paint, to paint the cans if desired

Scientific Information
Water moving inside a vibrating object causes the pitch to rise and fall. The relative size of the container also affects the pitch, with larger containers having lower sounds than smaller ones.

Sequence of Implementation
1. Start with one glissando can so that children can focus on the unusual sound created by the moving water.
2. Add a second can of a different size so children can compare the effect of size on the sound of the can.
3. Introduce a third size of can for comparison purposes.
4. Provide a can that is the same size as one of the other cans so children can compare their sounds.

What to Look For
Children will listen in fascination to the sound of the glissando
   cans.
Children will hold and shake the cans to try to determine what is
   causing the sounds.
Children will compare how the size of the cans affects the sound.

Questions to Extend Thinking
How does this instrument sound?
What do you think is making the sound?
Which glissando can has the highest sound?

Modification
Introduce a can that is identical to one of the others but does not
have the water. Children can compare its sound to that of the
cans with water.

Integrated Curriculum Activities
Let children make their own glissando cans. Ask parents to save
   the cans for you.
Demonstrate glissandos on other instruments, such as a keyboard
   or a dowel harp (activity 6.6).

Helpful Hint
The glissando cans can be suspended with heavy rubber bands or
pipe cleaners. Tape them to the cans if they slip off.

6.4 Block and Wood Block
Resonance

Description
This activity allows children to explore the concept of resonance in music. They can compare the sound of a wood block, which is hollow, to a similar block of wood that is solid. The wood block is a real musical instrument, and children will discover why.

Wood blocks are inexpensive and are readily available. They can also be easily made by using a piece of wood for the bottom (4 by 3 by 1 inches) and another piece of wood for the top (4 by 3 by ½ inches). Glue three small strips of wood to the bottom piece of wood, and glue the top in place. This creates a hollow area for resonance.

Which wood block has the nicest sound?

Child's Level
This activity is appropriate for either preschool or kindergarten children.

Materials
▲ wood block, either purchased or handmade
▲ block of wood, as close to the wood block in size and finish as possible
▲ wooden beater, made from a macramé bead with a 7-inch wooden dowel glued into the hole

Scientific Information
A hollow area is used to create resonance in musical instruments.

Sequence of Implementation
1. Put out both the wood block and block of wood in the music area so that children can compare the effect created by having a hollow area in the wood block.
2. Introduce wood blocks of other sizes, if desired. This allows children to compare the effect of size on the pitch of an instrument.

What to Look For
Children will play both the wood block and the block of wood and compare their sounds.
Some children will use the wood block to play rhythms.

Questions to Extend Thinking
How does the wood block sound?
How does the sound of the wood block compare to the sound of the piece of wood?

Modification
Wood blocks make excellent group-time instruments for playing rhythms. *See More Than Singing,* by Sally Moomaw, for ideas.

Integrated Curriculum Activities
Compare the wood block with other instruments made of wood, such as the dowel harp (activity 6.6) or the wooden rattle (activity 6.13).
Children may wish to make their own wood blocks. You can help them saw the wood and glue it together. Children can use rubber bands to hold their wood blocks together until they dry.

Helpful Hint
Wood blocks are inexpensive. Unless you already have wood left over from other projects, you may find that it is less expensive to buy a wood block than to make one.

6.5 Mallet Medley
Dynamics, Timbre

Description
Children quickly learn that each type of instrument has its own unique sound. Without experience, however, they may not realize that the type of mallet used to play an instrument also affects the sound. In this music center, children have the opportunity to play a wood block (activity 6.4) with five different types of mallets. They are all easily made.

Wooden—This is the most commonly used mallet. It is made from a macramé bead (¾ to 1 inch in diameter) and a wooden dowel. Choose a dowel that fits securely into the hole in the bead. Cut the dowel to a length of 7 inches. Use wood glue to secure the dowel to the inside of the bead. Wipe off any excess glue.

Hard Felt—This mallet produces a slightly softer sound than the wooden one. Make it exactly like the wooden mallet, but instead of wiping off the excess glue, place a small square of felt over the end of the bead and tie it in place around the bead. The glue will help hold the felt in place.

Soft Felt—This mallet makes a quieter sound than either the wood or hard felt mallets. Follow the instructions for the hard felt mallet, but add a layer of cotton balls or fiberfill in between the bead and the felt. This results in a softer surface and quieter tone.

Sponge—The sponge mallet is so soft that barely anything is heard, even if the child tries to play loudly. Cut a small piece of sponge, poke a hole in it, and glue it to a dowel.

Rubber—Rubber mallets make a resonant sound that is not as harsh as a wooden mallet. To make a rubber mallet, drill a hole in a hard rubber ball about 1 inch in diameter. Insert a 7-inch length of dowel into the hole and glue it in place.

Child's Level
This activity is appropriate for either preschool or kindergarten children.

Materials
▲ one or more wood blocks (see activity 6.4)
▲ mallets (described on page 208)

Scientific Information
The material of the mallet used to play an instrument affects both the timbre (tone quality) and how loud the instrument can sound.

Sequence of Implementation
1. Start with two beaters that sound very different, such as the wooden and the soft felt mallets.
2. Add additional types of mallets, one at a time, for comparison.

What to Look For
Children will experiment with how the different beaters sound on the wood block.
Children may try to hit the wood block harder with the soft mallets in an attempt to make a louder sound.

Questions to Extend Thinking
What happens when you switch beaters?
How does this beater feel? How does it sound?
Which beater makes the softest sound?

Modification
Children can try the different mallets on other instruments to see how they sound.

Integrated Curriculum Activities
If children have made their own wood blocks (see activity 6.4), they may wish to make some other types of mallets to go with them.
Use the mallets for a listening game at group time. Play them on an instrument behind a screen and let the children guess which mallet you are using.

Helpful Hint
Sand the cut edges of the dowels to avoid splinters.

6.6 Dowel Harps
Pitch

Description

The dowel harps give children an opportunity to explore the relationship between size and pitch in a wooden instrument. There are two types of dowel harps, both easily made.

One has ten dowels that are all ½ inch in diameter but vary in length, from 12 inches to 3 inches. (Each dowel is 1 inch shorter than the previous dowel.) The other dowel harp has ten dowels that are all the same length (8 inches) but vary in diameter from 1 inch down to ³⁄₁₆ inch.

For both dowel harps, drill holes the same size as the dowels and ¾ inch apart in a piece wood that is 1 inch thick, 3 inches wide, and 14 inches long. Glue the dowels into the holes. Attach strips of molding 6 inches long to the ends of the harp base; these strips add stability and help keep the dowel harp from tipping over.

What sounds can you make with the dowel harps?

Child's Level

This activity is appropriate for either preschool or kindergarten children.

Materials

▲ two dowel harps, as described above
▲ two wooden beaters, each made from a macramé bead with a 7-inch wooden dowel glued into the hole

Scientific Information

The size of a vibrating body affects its pitch. The larger the vibrating source, the lower the pitch. Variations in either length or width produce this effect, as can be demonstrated on the dowel harps.

Sequence of Implementation

1. Start with the dowel harp that varies in length so children can explore the effect that variations in length have on pitch.
2. Switch to the dowel harp that varies in diameter so children can explore the relationship between diameter and pitch.
3. Include both instruments in the center so children can play them together and compare the sounds.

What to Look For

Children will play the bars of the dowel harp and compare the
sounds.

Some children will construct the relationship between the length
or width of the bars and the relative pitch (high or low).

Children will sweep the beaters across all the bars, creating a glissando effect.

Many children will reverse the labels of high and low and call the
longest bar high because it extends higher in the air. You can
supply the appropriate labels.

Questions to Extend Thinking

What do you notice that's different about these bars?
What do you notice that's the same?
Which bar do I have to play to get the highest sound?
How does the widest bar sound?

Modification

Children can also play the dowel harps with beaters made from
different types of material to notice the effect that changing the
material has on the sound. Felt and hard rubber are possibilities
(see activity 6.5).

Integrated Curriculum Activities

Add dowel pieces to the block area for construction.
You can assist children in sawing lengths of dowel and constructing additional dowel harps.

Helpful Hint

Stain and varnish the dowel harps, if desired. In any case, be sure
to sand them so no one gets splinters.

6.7 Suspended Spoons
Pitch

Description
Suspended spoons have a resonant sound. Varying the size of the spoon affects the pitch. In this activity, children can tap spoons of different sizes with another spoon and compare how size affects pitch.

Child's Level
This activity is appropriate for either preschool or kindergarten children.

Materials
▲ spoons of assorted sizes
▲ wooden frame for suspending the spoons, or a pegboard divider with hooks

Scientific Information
The size of a vibrating object affects its pitch. Larger objects sound lower than smaller ones because they produce a lower number of vibrations per second.

Sequence of Implementation
1. Start with two spoons of the same size and one that is markedly different.
2. Introduce additional spoons of various sizes.

What to Look For
Children will play the spoons and listen to the sounds.

Some children will discover that the pitch varies with the size of the spoon.

Children may play all the spoons with a sweeping motion to create a glissando effect.

Some children may discover that the spoons sound more resonant when you tap them on the edge than when you tap the front or back of the bowl.

Questions to Extend Thinking
How can you use these spoons to create music?
Do any spoons sound the same?
Which spoon has the highest sound?

Modification
Try adding a slotted spoon. Many slotted spoons sound "thunky" because the number of holes decreases their resonance.

Integrated Curriculum Activities
Give children pairs of spoons to use to play the beats in songs or
  chants.
Use a variety of types of spoons with dry materials, such as rice,
  in the sensory table. Include containers to fill.

Helpful Hint
The spoons can be suspended by looping rubber bands around them and passing the end of the rubber band through its own loop to create a knot.

6.8 Sand Blocks
Timbre

Description
Sand blocks provide another opportunity for children to explore variations in tone quality, or timbre, among instruments. To make the sand blocks, use various grades of sandpaper, from course to very fine, and blocks of wood, 4 by 3 by ½ inches. Cover the bottom of each wood block with the sandpaper and wrap the sandpaper around the sides. Secure the sandpaper to the wood with glue, tacks, or a staple gun. You can screw knobs to the back of the sand blocks to make them easier to hold. Children play the instruments by scraping them together. The variations in sandpaper create differences in tone quality.

Child's Level
This activity is appropriate for either preschool or kindergarten children.

Materials
▲ several types of sand blocks, as described above

Scientific Information
Sound can be produced by scraping two things together, and some instruments are made to be scraped. The material used to make the instrument affects its timbre (tone color).

Sequence of Implementation
1. Start with three pairs of sand blocks: two pairs made from fine grain sandpaper and one pair made from course grain sandpaper. Children can compare the sand blocks made of the same material and contrast them with the sand blocks made from a different material.
2. Add one or more additional pairs of sandblocks from intermediate grades of sandpaper.

What to Look For
Children will scrape the sand blocks together to produce sounds.
Children will compare the sounds of the sand blocks.
Some children will notice that the sand blocks made of the same
type of sandpaper sound the same.

Questions to Extend Thinking
How can we use these instruments to make sounds?
Do all of the sand blocks sound the same?
Why does this pair of sand blocks sound different?

Modification
Children can also use sand blocks to accompany songs at
group time.

Integrated Curriculum Activities
Children can make their own sand blocks by gluing sandpaper to
pieces of wood.
Sand blocks often remind children of the sound of trains. Try
singing train songs as children experiment with the sand
blocks.

Helpful Hint
The sandpaper wears down with use and has to be replaced.

6.9 Surprise Box
Pitch

Description
The surprise box is unusual in both appearance and sound. Each side of this wooden box is a different height, so each side has a different pitch when tapped with a wooden mallet. The surprise box is made from ¼-inch thick wood, 8 inches wide, cut into lengths of 11, 9, 7, and 5 inches. The base is made from ½-inch thick wood to add stability. It is also 8 inches wide but is 6½ inches long. (Keep in mind that commercial 8-inch-wide wood is really only 7¼ inches wide.) Glue and nail the sides and the base together.

Child's Level
This activity is appropriate for either preschool or kindergarten children.

Materials
▲ wooden board as described above, or size desired
▲ wooden beater, made from a macramé bead with a 7-inch wooden dowel glued into the hole

Scientific Information
The size of a vibrating body affects its pitch. Although each side of the surprise box is made of wood, the sides all sound different because of their varying sizes. The longest side has the lowest pitch.

Sequence of Implementation
None required.

What to Look For

Children will tap the sides of the box and listen to the sounds.

Children will notice a relationship between the sizes of the wood and the resulting pitch.

Some children will be able to label the pitches high and low.

Some children will reverse the high and low labels because the longest side looks visually higher. You can supply the appropriate labels.

Some children will play rhythms on the box.

Questions to Extend Thinking

How do you think this box will sound when you play it?

Do the sides sound the same or different?

What is causing the changes in pitch?

Modification

Children can change the sound of the box by using different kinds of mallets. Try substituting felt or rubber beaters for experimentation (see activity 6.5).

Integrated Curriculum Activities

Children may enjoy other types of surprise boxes. Try hiding objects in small boxes and letting children guess what is inside.

A favorite end-of-the-year activity is "Pass the Box." A small item for each child in the class is placed in a surprise box. The box is wrapped in many layers of paper, with one layer for each child in the class. Pass the box around the group time circle as music plays. Each time the music stops, whoever is holding the box can open it. Each child in the class can have a chance to open the surprise box!

Helpful Hint

Any type of wood will create different pitches when cut to varying lengths. Try to select a hard wood if possible because of the more resonant tone.

6.10 Nature's Maracas
Timbre

Description
Natural materials can make lovely maracas. In this activity, children can experiment with shaking locust pods, lotus pods, and dried gourds of various types. You can use materials indigenous to your own area. An addition to this music center is the *shekere,* an African instrument made from a dried gourd, with a net of beans tied around the outside of the gourd.

Child's Level
This activity is appropriate for either preschool or kindergarten children.

Materials
- ▲ natural materials that produce a sound when shaken, such as dried gourds, lotus pods, and locust pods
- ▲ shekere, an African instrument

Scientific Information
Many natural materials produce a rattling sound after they dry out.

Sequence of Implementation
1. Start with the gourds. Include some gourds that are fresh and some that are dried out. Children can compare how they sound.
2. Add other natural materials that produce a sound when shaken, such as lotus pods or locust pods.
3. Introduce the shekere, which is a special adaptation of a dried gourd. It is very intriguing to children.

What to Look For
Children will shake the materials and listen to the sounds.
Children will feel the materials and speculate about what is making the sounds.
Children will compare the sounds of the maracas.
Some children may use the maracas to accompany singing.

Questions to Extend Thinking
What happens when you shake these things?
What could be making the sound?
Why does this gourd make a sound and this one doesn't?

Modification
Try to collect enough of one type of material to use for maracas at group time. Children can accompany songs with the maracas. See *More Than Singing*, by Sally Moomaw, for songs to use with maracas.

Integrated Curriculum Activities
Take a nature walk and look for natural materials to use as instruments.
Read *Max Found Two Sticks*, by Brian Pinkney, or similar books. A boy in this book finds a musical use for natural items.
Have children make guesses about what is making the sounds inside the maracas and write down their observations. Then open some of the materials as a special activity to see what is inside.

Helpful Hint
Look in craft stores if the natural materials used as maracas are not indigenous to your area. Lotus pods are commonly available.

6.11 Maraca Fillers
Timbre, Dynamics

Description
The filler of a maraca affects not only the tone color of the instrument but also how loudly the instrument can be played. Children can discover these properties of sound in this activity. The containers used for the maracas are clear plastic jars. They make a resonant sound and also allow children to see what is inside producing the sound. The maraca fillers—beans, rice, and cornmeal—make very different sounds when shaken. They also differ markedly in how loud they sound. Children typically think that dynamics is determined solely by how hard they strike, strum, or shake an instrument. This activity helps them understand other factors that affect dynamics.

Child's Level
This activity is appropriate for either preschool or kindergarten children.

Materials
▲ clear plastic jars and lids
▲ beans, rice, and cornmeal for fillers

Scientific Information
The type of material used to fill a maraca affects both the tone quality and how loud the instrument sounds.

Sequence of Implementation
1. Start with three maracas with markedly different sounds so that children can easily compare them.
2. Add one or two maracas that duplicate fillers in the maracas already present so children can observe that the same filler makes the same sound in both maracas.
3. Introduce additional maracas with different fillers for exploration.

What to Look For
Children will shake the maracas and look carefully at the fillers to
    determine what is making the sounds.
Children will compare the sounds of the maracas.
Children will notice that some maracas sound louder than others.
Children will shake the soft maracas extra hard to try to make
    them sound louder.
Some children will sing or move along with the maracas.

Questions to Extend Thinking
What is making the sound?
Which maraca should I use if I want to play loudly?
Is there any way to make the cornmeal maraca loud?
What else could we put in the maracas that would make them
    loud?

Modification
Children may want to suggest fillers for additional maracas to use
in the center.

Integrated Curriculum Activities
Make a set of maracas to use at group time. Rice is a good choice
    since it is not too loud but can be heard by the children.
Let the children make their own maracas. Ask parents to donate
    plastic jars.

Helpful Hint
Glue the tops on the containers or children will mix the contents
and will no longer be able to compare sounds.

6.12 Maraca Containers
Timbre, Dynamics

Description
It is not only the filler of a maraca that affects the sound of the instrument; the material of the container also impacts both tone quality and dynamics. This activity is an excellent follow-up to activity 6.11, "Maraca Fillers." It enables children to understand the relationship between the container of a maraca and the sound it produces.

Child's Level
This activity is appropriate for either preschool or kindergarten children.

Materials
- ▲ aluminum can, plastic jar, and a cardboard salt box to use for maraca containers
- ▲ additional types of containers
- ▲ rice, for filler

Scientific Information
The material of the container of a maraca affects both the tone quality of the instrument and how loud it sounds.

Sequence of Implementation
1. Start with three maracas made from containers that are approximately the same size but are made of different materials. Partially fill each maraca with rice.
2. Add a second set of maracas exactly like the first set. Children can observe that maracas made with the same containers and fillers sound the same.
3. Introduce maracas with rice filler but additional varieties of containers for experimentation.

What to Look For
Children will shake the maracas and listen to the sounds.
Children may need to be told that all of the maracas have rice
  fillers since they cannot see inside all of the containers.
Children will compare the sounds of the different maracas.
Children will notice that some maracas sound louder than others.
Children may shake the cardboard maraca harder to make it
  sound louder.
Some children will sing along with the maracas.

Questions to Extend Thinking
How do these maracas sound?
What makes them sound different?
Which maraca has the softest sound?
Is there any way to make the can maraca sound soft?
If you made a maraca, what would you use to make it?

Modification
Once children have had the opportunity to explore separately the
impact of the filler and container on the sound of a maraca, they
may wish to experiment with how both factors interact. This can
be done in either the music center or as a special activity. Provide
several types of containers and allow children to experiment with
trying a variety of fillers in them.

Integrated Curriculum Activities
Let the children make their own maracas. They can suggest containers and fillers, and parents can help you assemble the necessary supplies.
Use maracas to accompany songs or movements at group time.

Helpful Hint
Color the salt box the same color as the aluminum can so that
children do not think that the differences in sound are related to
the color of the container.

6.13 Rattle Quintet
Timbre, Dynamics

Description
This activity allows children to experiment with five types of rattles and compare the sounds. One instrument comes from West Africa and is made of dried gourd slices encircling a stick. A second instrument consists of circular wooden disks mounted on a tooled wooden shaft. Contrasting instruments include a plastic baby rattle, a metal rattle made from juice lids, and a soft foam rattle.

To make the metal rattle, drill holes in the center of the juice lids and mount them on a dowel. Glue beads to both ends to keep the disks from falling off the stick.

To make a soft-sounding rattle, mount foam replacement disks from a Space Shooter toy to a wooden dowel. Glue beads to the ends of the dowel, as with the metal rattle.

Child's Level
This activity is appropriate for either preschool or kindergarten children.

Materials
▲ assorted rattles, as described above
▲ rattles made from additional materials, as desired

Scientific Information
The material an instrument is made from affects its timbre (tone quality) and how loud or soft it sounds.

Sequence of Implementation
1. Start with several rattles so that children can examine the material they are made from and compare the sounds.
2. Add an instrument that is identical to one in the first group. Children can observe that instruments made of the same material sound the same.
3. Introduce rattles made from additional materials for further exploration.

What to Look For
Children will shake the rattles and listen to the sounds.

Children will compare the sounds of the rattles.

Children will notice that the rattles are made from different materials.

Some children will form relationships between the material used to make the rattle and the sound of the instrument.

Questions to Extend Thinking
How do these instruments work?

Which rattles sound the most alike?

What do you think we could use to make a soft-sounding rattle?

Modification
Children may have ideas for additional rattles to make for the center. Wooden or plastic beads, pasta wheels, plastic lids with holes cut in the center, and felt circles are some of the many possibilities. The use of softer materials, such as plastic lids or felt, allows children to explore dynamic changes related to the materials.

Integrated Curriculum Activities
Use jingle sticks at group time to play the beats of a song. Jingle sticks have metal disks mounted on a stick and are thus a type of metal rattle.

The rattles go well with a baby theme in the classroom.

Helpful Hint
After drilling the holes in the metal disks, file the edges so they are not sharp.

6.14 Clay Disks
Pitch, Timbre

Description
Clay saucers from flower pots make lovely sounding instruments when suspended so they can vibrate freely. An assortment of sizes allows children to once again explore the relationship between size and pitch in music and science. Carefully drill a small hole in the center of each clay saucer. Suspend the disks individually or hang several on the same cord. Knot a small bead below each saucer to hold them in place.

Child's Level
This activity is most appropriate for older preschool or kindergarten children.

Materials
▲ clay saucers from flower pots
▲ cord or fishing line
▲ small beads
▲ wooden beaters, each made from a macramé bead with a 7-inch wooden dowel glued into the hole

Scientific Information
Clay can be a resonant sounding medium. As with other vibrating bodies, the size of the instrument affects its pitch. The larger disks sound lower than the smaller ones.

Sequence of Implementation
1. Start with several saucers that vary in size.
2. Add additional disks, including some that are the same size.

What to Look For

Children will play the disks and listen to the pleasing sounds.
Children will compare the sizes of the disks with differences
   in pitch.
Some children will be able to label high and low sounds.

Questions to Extend Thinking

What do you notice about the sounds of these clay saucers?
Do any saucers sound the same?
What happens when you play the biggest disk?

Modification

Children can also use flower pots as instruments. They can be
easily suspended through the hole in the bottom of the pot.

Integrated Curriculum Activities

This activity coordinates well with spring planting themes.
   Children can use flower pots to plant seeds.
Read books about children experimenting with found materials
   for instruments. *Max, the Music-Maker,* by Miriam B. Strecher
   and Alice S. Kandell, and *Max Found Two Sticks,* by Brian
   Pinkney, are examples.

Helpful Hint

If you mount several disks on the same cord, place the smallest
disk on top. This helps children associate the high pitch label
with the smaller instrument, which is mounted higher.

6.15 Shell Sounds
Timbre

Description
Shells can be used to produce musical sounds in several ways. Some shells can be strung together to form wind chimes; others can be mounted on a cord to form a rattle. Shells with ridges, such as scallops, can be scraped to produce sounds. This center encourages children to explore shells for creating interesting sounds and music.

Child's Level
This activity is most appropriate for older preschool and kindergarten children.

Materials
- ▲ seashell wind chimes, as pictured
- ▲ woven fans
- ▲ bellows
- ▲ small shells mounted on cords to form rattles
- ▲ scallops, or other shells with ridges, for scraping

Scientific Information
Shells can be used to produce musical sounds by tapping them together, shaking them together as a rattle, or scraping them. The physical features of the shell determine its musical use.

Sequence of Implementation
1. Start with the wind chimes and a woven fan. Children can use the fan to move the air, thus creating sounds with the shells.
2. Add the bellows as another way to move air and thus play the chimes.
3. Introduce the shell rattles. Children can compare how they produce sound with rattles and wind chimes.
4. Add several pairs of shells for scraping.

What to Look For
Children will move the shell chimes with their fingers as well as by moving the air.
Children will listen to the sounds created by the different varieties of shells.
Children will experiment with scraping the shells to create sound.

Questions to Extend Thinking
How can we make music with these shells?
How can you make the wind chimes move without touching them?

Modification
Consider introducing a pair of shells that look like the ridged shells but are smooth. Children can contrast the effect of scraping a smooth shell with the sound produced by a serrated shell.

Integrated Curriculum Activities
Put a variety of shells in the science area for exploration (activity 2.13).
Create a shell collection for sorting and classifying. See *More Than Counting,* by Sally Moomaw and Brenda Hieronymus, activity 3.8.
Read books about shells and sea life.

Helpful Hint
Parents are an excellent source of shells. Shells are now often available in odd-lot or dollar stores.

6.16 Water Glasses
Pitch

Description
This activity allows children to experiment with the effect raising and lowering the level of water in a glass has on its pitch. Children can pour the water from a pitcher into the glasses and tap them with a spoon to determine the sound. They can pour water back and forth from pitcher to glasses for repeated explorations. If the glasses and pitcher are contained on a tray, this activity is much less messy than might be imagined.

Child's Level
This activity is most appropriate for older preschool and kindergarten children.

Materials
▲ two water glasses
▲ small pitcher of water
▲ spoon
▲ tray with raised sides

Scientific Information
As the amount of water in a glass increases, the pitch becomes lower. When the glass is tapped, the column of water vibrates. The larger the column of water, the lower the number of vibrations per second and the lower the pitch.

Sequence of Implementation
1. Start with two glasses so children can pour the water to different levels and compare the sounds.
2. Add additional glasses so children can compare more pitches.

What to Look For

Children will add water to the glasses and tap them to hear the
    sound.
Children will pour the water back and forth between the glasses
    and the pitcher.
After a period of exploration, some children will discover that the
    height of the water affects the pitch.
Some children may try to sing along as they play the glasses.

Questions to Extend Thinking

What happens to the sound when you pour water into the
    glasses?
Can you make the glasses sound the same?
What do I have to do to make this glass sound lower?

Modification

Tape marks can be added to the glasses at the levels needed to
create a scale.

Integrated Curriculum Activity

Put plastic pitchers and jars in the sensory table for additional
pouring opportunities.

Helpful Hint

Be sure the glasses you select are the same pitch. Variations in
the thickness of the glass can cause some glasses to vary in pitch
before the water is added and negate the learning value of this
activity.

$6./7$ Bottle Scale
Pitch

Description
The bottle scale is an excellent follow-up to experimenting with water glasses (activity 6.16). In this activity, glass bottles are filled with water to the depth necessary to create a scale. The bottles are then sealed shut. Children can use the bottles to explore the relationship between the height of the water and the pitch. They can also play tunes on the bottles.

Child's Level
This activity is most appropriate for older preschool and kindergarten children.

Materials
▲ glass bottles
▲ water (colored with food coloring, if desired)
▲ wooden beater, made from a macramé bead with a 7-inch wooden dowel glued into the hole

Scientific Information
The size of a vibrating body affects its pitch. Larger instruments sound lower than smaller instruments. Regulating the height of the vibrating column can be used to produce a musical scale.

Sequence of Implementation
1. Start with the water glass activity (6.16), if appropriate for your group.
2. After children have experimented with varying the depth of water to alter the sound of the glasses, introduce the bottle scale.
3. Add a second bottle scale that is identical to the first. Children can compare how bottles with the same water level sound.

What to Look For
Children will play the bottles and compare their sounds.
Some children may play tunes on the bottles.
Some children may use the bottles to make up songs.

Questions to Extend Thinking
What can you do with these bottles?
Which bottle should I play to make a higher sound?
Which bottle has the lowest sound?

Modification
You may wish to model playing a simple song such as "Mary Had a Little Lamb" on the bottle scale to give children the idea that the water bottles can be used to play a tune.

Integrated Curriculum Activities
Use the bottle scale to accompany songs at group time.
Put small bottles and eyedroppers in the water table (activity 4.11).

Helpful Hint
Ten to twelve-ounce bottles are a good size for making a five-note scale.

6.18 Alumiphone
Pitch

Description
The alumiphone produces a beautiful sound. It is made from lengths of 1-inch aluminum piping cut so that each bar is slightly shorter than the previous bar. The slight variance in length results in a tuning that is *microtonal*, meaning that the pitches are closer together than two adjacent keys on the piano. Many cultures around the world create microtonal music; this instrument allows children to explore those possibilities. Mount the alumiphone on a dense foam frame made from packing material. Cut grooves into the foam to hold the bars.

Child's Level
This activity is appropriate for either preschool or kindergarten children.

Materials
▲ alumiphone instrument, as described above
▲ hard rubber mallet, made by drilling a hole into a small rubber ball and gluing a 7-inch dowel into the hole

Scientific Information
The size of a vibrating body affects its pitch. Small changes in length result in slight changes in pitch. The longer bars sound lower than the shorter bars.

Sequence of Implementation
1. Introduce children to the concept of pitch and its relationship to size through an instrument with very clear-cut size and pitch differences. Two sizes of triangles (activity 6.1) or the dowel harp (activity 6.6) are possibilities.
2. After children have had some experiences exploring the relationship between size and pitch, introduce the alumiphone, which has smaller size and pitch gradations.

What to Look For

Children will play the alumiphone and listen to its lovely sound.

Children will sweep the beater along the bars to create a glissando effect.

Some children will notice that the bars differ slightly in size and sound.

Some children will try to play tunes on the alumiphone and discover that it is not a traditional Western scale.

Some children will create music on the alumiphone.

Questions to Extend Thinking

What can you play on this instrument?

How does the alumiphone sound?

Do all the bars sound the same?

Do the bars next to each other sound the same?

Modification

Children may wish to try other types of mallets on the alumiphone after they have had experience playing it with the rubber beater. Wooden and felt mallets are possibilities (see activity 6.5).

Integrated Curriculum Activity

Provide background music for children to listen to that uses microtonality. Music from India is one source. Check the international section in music stores to find music from India as well as other countries.

Helpful Hints

The aluminum piping can be cut with a saw. Be sure to file the edges so they are not sharp.

Copper and steel pipes also make lovely instruments.

6.19 String Stretcher
Pitch

Description

Children often have less experience with string instruments than with percussion instruments. This activity allows them to experiment with strings. An important factor that affects the pitch of a string is the tension on it. The tighter a string is stretched, the higher the pitch. It is this phenomenon that is used to tune string instruments. This music center includes three devices that enable children to experiment with the effect of string tension on pitch: a string stretcher, a string tension device (for comparing loose and tight strings), and a string tightener.

The string stretcher allows children to manipulate a moveable axle peg (a narrow dowel with a wide base) in order to stretch a rubber band; they can observe the effect on pitch when they pluck it. To make this device, insert a screw or wooden peg into a wooden base (3 by 12 inches) about 1 inch from one end of the base. Glue narrow strips of wood (¼ inch thick) to the top of the base at both ends. Next, form the top of the frame by gluing two strips of wood (1 by 12 inches, ¼ inch thick) to the wood strips already attached to the base. Position the top wood pieces just far enough apart to create a slit so that the axle peg can slide back and forth without its wide end coming out of the groove. Loop a rubber band over the two pegs. Children can stretch the rubber band by sliding the axle peg across the frame. The rubber band rises in pitch as it becomes tighter.

When children stretch rubber bands, it appears that as the string gets longer, it goes up in pitch. Children cannot easily observe that the string also becomes narrower in width as it stretches. In order to help children understand that it is the tightness of the string that is affecting the pitch, the string tension device enables children to compare two strings of the same length, one tight and the other loose. The strings are stretched across a wooden base (3 by 12 inches) and attached to screws at both ends. Children can observe how the varying tension on the strings alters the pitch.

The string tightener allows children to turn a knob to tighten the tension on fishing line. Secure a piece of fishing line to a screw attached to the end of a wooden base (3 by 12 inches). Attach the other end of the fishing line to a turnable knob mounted at the opposite end of the frame. As children turn the knob, the fishing line wraps around the knob and becomes tighter, thus rising in pitch.

Child's Level
This activity is most appropriate for older preschool or kinder-garten children.

Materials
▲ string stretching devices, as described above

Scientific Information
As strings become more taut, they go up in pitch.

Sequence of Implementation
1. Start with the string stretcher, which allows children to stretch a rubber band. Children can observe a greater connection between their action of stretching the string and the change in pitch with this device.
2. Add the frame with the tight and loose strings. Children can compare how the tightness of the string affects its pitch.
3. Introduce the string tightener device. Children can make the string tighter without the string appearing to increase in length.

What to Look For
Children will be intrigued with stretching the strings and listening to the changes in pitch.

Do not expect children to fully understand these concepts. These are beginning explorations.

Questions to Extend Thinking
What can you do with this device?
What happens to the string when you stretch it?
How does the string sound after you stretch it?

Modification
Children can stretch rubber bands by hooking them over their shoes to make a crude string instrument to use at group time.

Integrated Curriculum Activity
Use rubber bands with geoboards in the manipulative area.

Helpful Hint
Wire can be used instead of fishing line for the second device.

6.20 Lap Harps
Pitch

Description
The three lap harps used in this music center enable children to explore how the length, width, and tension of strings affect pitch.

The first lap harp has strings that are the same thickness but vary in length. It is made by stretching fishing line across screw eyes screwed into a base of wood. The screw eyes allow the strings to be tightened or loosened for tuning purposes.

The second lap harp has strings that are the same length but vary in width. It is made by stretching rubber bands of varying thicknesses across nails hammered into a piece of wood. The nails are all equal distance apart, so the strings are the same length. A commercial lap harp is also included in this music center. Children can create beautiful music with lap harps.

"The Music Maker" pictured here by Peeleman/McLaughlin Enterprises Inc.

Child's Level
This activity is most appropriate for older preschool or kindergarten children.

Materials
▲ lap harps, as described above

Scientific Information
Several factors affect the pitch of string instruments: the length of the strings, the width of the strings, and the tension on the strings.

Sequence of Implementation
1. Start with the lap harp with strings of varying length.
2. Switch to the lap harp with strings of varying width.
3. Introduce the commercial lap harp, if available. All three lap harps can be used in the music center at this time.

What to Look For
Children will pluck the strings and listen to the sounds.
Children will observe differences among the strings.
Some children will construct relationships between the dimensions of the strings and their pitch.
Some children will attempt to play tunes on the lap harps.

Questions to Extend Thinking

How can you play this instrument?
What is making the sound?
Do you notice any differences among the strings?
What is making the pitches different among these strings?

Modification

Children can play the lap harp with various types of picks, if desired. Plastic, felt, and metal picks are available.

Integrated Curriculum Activities

Plan for a demonstration of other string instruments, if possible.
Play recordings of plucked string instruments for children to listen to as they interact with the lap harps.

Helpful Hints

Be sure to regulate the tension on the strings of the lap harps. If the tension is not equal on the strings, a longer or thicker string could have a higher pitch than a shorter or thinner one.
Try to use rubber bands that are all the same color so children don't think changes in pitch are due to the color of the rubber bands.

Science in Cooking

Yuan-shang turned the handle on the apple peeler. At first he had difficulty, but then he turned the handle rhythmically and squealed with delight as the apple peelings fell into a pile at the end of the peeler. His teacher gathered the pieces and gave Yuan-shang a child-safe knife so that he could chop the apple into smaller pieces. The teacher cooked the apple for a taste test, during which the children tasted processed applesauce and the applesauce they made. The results of the taste test were placed on a graph at group time. The children commented on the texture, color, and flavor of each type of applesauce, thus participating in several components of the scientific process: observation, comparison, classification, and communication.

▲ ▲ ▲

Megan's father reported that one of her favorite snacks was a fruit drink made with yogurt. He expressed his concern about sugary foods and suggested this as an alternative. The teacher planned to make fruit smoothies as a cooking activity and invited Megan's father to assist. The children used knives to cut strawberries and bananas. They poured orange juice from a pitcher into a measuring cup, spooned yogurt into a separate cup, and the teacher combined the mixture in a blender. She gave each child a portion to taste. The children used a wedge (knife), observed whole to part changes, measured, created a new mixture, and observed the changes after the addition of ice to the blender. They also tasted the individual components of the recipe and the combination of the parts in the final product.

▲ ▲ ▲

Children observe parents and caregivers preparing food from the time they are able to sit in the kitchen. They eagerly await the preparation of their bottles, for example, or recognize the process for making cereal. They pull up a chair and stand next to the adults as they cook. In many cases food preparation at home is not a safe activity for children; however, the process can be both safe and valuable in early childhood programs. Children explore the physical properties of both foods and cooking implements. They are independent in the uses of some simple tools and they create many scientific relationships, such as "If I do this, then this happens" or "What happens next?"

Teachers' Questions
What cooking activities promote the scientific process?

Cooking activities in which children actively participate encourage them to closely observe, predict, infer, compare, measure, classify, communicate, and create relationships. Cooking activities, by nature, involve either the movement of objects, changes in materials, or both. For example, stirring flavor crystals to make Jell-O involves the movement of a tool. Changes occur in the mixture, and dry and wet materials mix to form a solution. Further changes occur when the mixture is placed into the refrigerator. The teacher plans activities that optimize children's involvement and create opportunities to observe changes and the movement of objects.

What cooking activities involve the movement of objects?

Cooking activities that allow children to handle the ingredients and manipulate hand tools enhance children's understanding of the movement of objects. Developmentally appropriate cooking activities are designed to involve children to the fullest extent. For example, children might cut fruit with a plastic knife to make a fruit salad, or they could turn the crank on a food mill to produce squashed apples for making applesauce. Children use their bodies to create the movement and therefore receive immediate feedback from the tool or the materials. Some fruits are easier to cut than others and the effort needed to squash the apples is lessened as more of the apples are pushed through the mesh in the mill.

What cooking activities involve changes in materials?

All cooking activities involve changes in materials or a change in state, such as solid to liquid or uncooked to cooked. Cooking activities provide children with a myriad of opportunities for participation in the scientific process. The child who observes that Jell-O crystals combine with water to create a new solution may infer that all materials will respond in the same manner. This hypothesis will be tested in the sandbox as the same child experiments with mixing sand and water. The results are quite different than expected. Thus the child must continue to think about the formation of solutions.

Why is it important to include cooking activities that promote the scientific process?

The exploration of the movement of objects and changes in materials that occur during cooking activities help lay a foundation for the understanding of physics and chemistry. Through the use of a hand chopper to cut onions, children discover that the force of several blades (wedges) makes the work easier than it would otherwise be. Children also observe a physical change in the onions. As the onions are chopped, the pungent aroma is released for all to experience.

Also, cooking is a part of all cultures and a familiar home experience for children.

What scientific principles emerge as children participate in cooking activities?

Scientific principles related to physics and chemistry emerge in developmentally appropriate, child-centered cooking activities. The hands-on exploration of the materials furthers the children's cognitive development and interest as they create relationships among the materials they use. For example, as children combine flour with eggs and milk, they observe the change as a solution is created. This is chemistry! As children use a knife to cut a potato, work is made easier through use of a simple machine, a wedge. This is physics! The scientific principles specific to each activity are noted on the individual activities of this chapter.

What relationships can children create through participation in cooking activities?

Children create relationships between their actions on objects and the reactions of the materials. They also explore how cooking implements affect the ingredients and how the ingredients react with one another when combined. Repeated experiences with the same and/or similar implements and ingredients increase the likelihood that children will create such relationships. In the individual activities in this chapter, you will find suggestions for sequencing the cooking activities or for related cooking activities that help children create relationships.

What is wrong with the cooking activities in traditional cookbooks for children?

Cookbooks for children rarely, if ever, focus on the scientific knowledge that emerges during the cooking experience, even though the activities themselves may be developmentally appropriate. Cookbooks typically identify language development goals (such as introduction of new vocabulary) or math concepts (such as measurement) as the learning opportunities. The activities in this chapter are similar to many traditional experiences, but they go a step further to help teachers identify the science potential of the experiences.

What cooking implements are needed to encourage scientific thinking?

Commonly used kitchen tools are an important component of the science curriculum integrated into cooking activities. Teachers often introduce spoons, spatulas, and eggbeaters for cooking activities. In addition, teachers may use blenders, electric mixers, and juicers for cooking experiences. We suggest that teachers substitute hand mixers, juicers, and other hand tools whenever possible to increase the potential for scientific learning. These tools give children experiences with simple machines and allow greater opportunities for the construction of physical knowledge, since children directly operate the tools. Other implements include wire whisks, pastry and pizza wheels, hand choppers and grinders, potato mashers, and old-fashioned apple peelers.

Where can teachers find the equipment needed to encourage scientific thinking during cooking activities?

The cooking tools may already be a part of the equipment teachers have, or they may be purchased at a reasonable price. Parents and grandparents, discount stores, garage sales, and flea markets are also valuable resources for the hand tools needed for cooking experiences.

How often do teachers plan specific cooking activities?

Some teachers plan a cooking activity once a week, while others may be limited to cooking once a month. Regardless of the frequency of these experiences, teachers often choose to plan the cooking activity to coordinate with some aspect of the total curriculum. The teacher might plan to mash potatoes after using the potato mashers as a painting implement (activity 5.6). The teacher could plan to cook vegetable soup to coordinate with a farmer's market in the dramatic play area and the book *Growing Vegetable Soup,* by Lois Ehlert.

How do teachers organize and set up the cooking activities?

Teachers can set up cooking activities in stations or as small group activities. The organization and set up are determined by the number of children involved and the number of adults available to assist. One way to set up the activity is to plan stations for each step of the process. For example, when making toast, the teacher plans three stations on the table. At the first station a recipe card instructs the child to place one slice of bread in the toaster and remove the finished product with toast tongs. An adult would supervise this part of the process. The recipe card at the second station instructs the child to spread the toast with butter. Finally, at the third station, the recipe card shows a picture of a child eating toast and the directions are, "Eat the toast for snack."

A second organizational method is the small group approach. The teacher sets up a special table for three to four children at a time to participate in the cooking activity. Groups of children rotate through the activity until all children have had an opportunity to participate. A waiting list helps children more easily delay participation and allows the teacher to keep track of who has had a turn already. Cooking involves a substantial commitment in time and effort, but the results are rewarding for teacher and children!

How can teachers assess children's understanding of scientific concepts related to the movement of objects and the changes in materials?

Teachers can record anecdotal records based on observation of children during cooking activities. This is probably easier than trying to record data on a checklist because the responses will be very individual to specific children and experiences. The teacher can use information gathered from many different areas of the classroom to determine whether the child is able to create relationships and/or notice the changes in materials.

Cooking
Activities

7.1 Soup for Lunch
Vegetable Soup

Description

While cooking vegetable soup, children observe raw vegetables and change them in several ways. They wash them, peel or scrape them if necessary, and cut them with a child-safe knife. A few ingredients, such as onions and spinach, can be chopped. The teacher may have to cut some hard vegetables into manageable pieces or assist some children in using the knives. After the vegetables are prepared for cooking, the teacher adds tomato juice and spices and then boils the mixture. Additional changes in the vegetables occur during cooking.

Child's Level

Making vegetable soup is appropriate for preschool and kindergarten children. Older, more experienced children can assume more responsibility for planning the selection of vegetables to include.

Materials

- ▲ potatoes, celery, turnips, carrots, green beans, zucchini, onions, or other vegetables
- ▲ spices, such as basil, salt, and pepper
- ▲ canned tomato juice or V-8 juice to make the broth
- ▲ child-safe knives (often called pumpkin knives)
- ▲ hand chopper for the onion

Scientific Information

Vegetables can be changed from whole into parts and from raw to cooked. The application of heat changes the hardness, the texture, the color, and in some instances, the taste.

Sequence of Implementation

1. Vegetable soup can be prepared at a table set up for four or five children at a time. As children finish cutting the vegetables, other children can sit at an empty place. Offer children a choice of which vegetables to cut and allow them to taste the raw vegetables. Talk about the similarities and differences in the vegetables as well as the ease or difficulty of cutting them.

2. All the ingredients go into one pot for cooking.
3. The teacher adds the spices and the tomato juice and cooks the
     soup in a microwave or on a stovetop. Enjoy the soup for
     lunch or invite parents to attend a pot luck dinner that
     evening. The children have prepared the main dish!

What to Look For
Children may experience some initial difficulty using the knives
    to cut hard vegetables. You can assist children in the process.
Some children may use the wrong edge of the knife.
Some children may be more interested in eating than cutting.
    Others may want to cut all the vegetables. You can limit the
    quantities of vegetables you give each child.
Many children may be unfamiliar with the raw form of some veg-
    etables and need you to supply the names for them.

Questions to Extend Thinking
Which vegetable is the hardest to cut?
How does the potato feel?
Is there any other vegetable that looks like the turnip?
Do you think the turnip will look the same after it is cooked?

Integrated Curriculum Activities
Include the book *Growing Vegetable Soup,* by Lois Ehlert, in the
    reading area.
Grow your own vegetables and use them in the soup.
Make other kinds of soup.
Plan to use vegetables as printing tools for an art activity.
Take a field trip to a local farmer's market or grocery store to pur-
    chase the vegetables.
Have the children vote for their favorite vegetable. Graph the
    results.

Helpful Hint
Plastic knives will not cut hard vegetables. If the knives break,
they may injure a child.

7.2 Peel and Chop
Homemade Applesauce

Description
This cooking activity provides excellent opportunities for children to find out more about apples. They wash them and use an old-fashioned hand peeler to remove the skin and core as well as slice the apples. The children chop the slices in a hand chopper, and the teacher cooks the small pieces in either a microwave or on the stovetop. Use the applesauce as a snack or add it to the lunch menu.

Child's Level
This activity is appropriate for preschool and kindergarten children.

Materials
- ▲ enough apples for each child to have one
- ▲ one or more old-fashioned apple peelers
- ▲ one or more hand choppers
- ▲ a large pot or bowls for cooking the applesauce
- ▲ microwave or stove (a hot plate could also be used)
- ▲ cinnamon, if desired

Scientific Information
The work of peeling, coring, and slicing the apple is made easier by the use of the apple peeler. Physical changes occur in the apple as the skin and core are removed. The apples change from whole to parts when sliced. Additional changes take place with the application of heat to cook the apples. The process of cooking breaks down the apple fibers, which become softer and change color.

Sequence of Implementation
1. Set up this activity in stations in order to keep several children involved at once. This activity takes a while to complete. You will probably need some extra hands to help with groups of younger children.
2. The first station is the apple peeler. Children can accomplish this part independently after you place the apple onto the prongs of the holder. The apple will be peeled, cored, and sliced.

3. Place the slices into a bowl and move to station two—the hand chopper. With some minor assistance in securing the lid, children can also do this independently.
4. The last step in the process involves cooking the apples, which you do in the classroom or kitchen, if available.
5. After the applesauce is cooked, children can add cinnamon, if desired, and then eat the applesauce for a snack or save it for lunch.

What to Look For

Children will be very excited about the apple peeler. Be prepared for a long waiting list and a large audience of observers!

Children are also fascinated with the hand chopper. They enjoy the powerful feeling as their actions cause the movement of the chopper.

Some children may engage in the cooking activity but not eat the applesauce.

Children will observe that the inside of the apple is a different color from the outside.

Questions to Extend Thinking

What does this tool do?

How does the peel look when it comes off of the apple?

Is the inside of your apple the same color as the outside?

Integrated Curriculum Activities

Plan other applesauce activities, such as tasting uncooked applesauce or applesauce made from other varieties of apples.

Make applesauce without removing the skin from the apples.

Plan a taste test of processed and homemade applesauce.

Graph the results of the taste test.

Use apples as a printing tool for an art activity.

Use the apple peeler to remove the skin from potatoes.

Helpful Hint

Use hard, evenly shaped apples for easier peeling.

7.3 Juice for Snack
Squeezing Orange Juice

Description
The use of a hand juicer gives children another experience in using a lever to make work easier. This is an extension of activities with the lever found in chapter 3, "Machines and Pendulums." They observe the whole orange, the halves of the orange, and the results of squeezing out all the juice. They also taste the juice of the orange.

Child's Level
This activity is appropriate for older preschool and kindergarten children. Younger children may not have enough strength to operate the juicer.

Materials
- ▲ one or more hand juicers, as shown
- ▲ enough oranges (cut in half) for each child to squeeze two halves
- ▲ cups for collecting the juice

Scientific Information
More juice can be squeezed from the orange by using a machine than by using your hands. When the child pushes the handle (lever) down, the force is concentrated on the orange and the juice is forced through a hole and into the cup. Less pressure is needed to push down the handle as more of the juice is forced out of the orange. The orange goes through two physical changes, first when cut in half and again when the juice is squeezed out.

Sequence of Implementation
This activity is easy to implement because it is easy to set up and because it moves along quickly. Children do not have to wait a long time for a turn, and only one step is involved in the process. Cleanup is also easy. You need assist only by cutting the oranges into halves. The cut oranges can be prepared ahead of time.

What to Look For

Children will be very curious about the odd-looking machine. You
    may have a crowd gather to watch other children squeeze juice.
Some children may want to squeeze and squeeze and squeeze.
    You can limit how many oranges each child may use.
A few children may choose not to participate, but rather observe.

Questions to Extend Thinking

What is inside the orange?
What happens when you lift the handle?
How will you close the lid?
What happened when you pushed on the handle?
Is there another way to get the juice out of the orange?

Integrated Curriculum Activities

Compare different brands of orange juice.
Estimate how many seeds are inside an orange.
Make lemonade with the hand juicer.
Include a fruit and vegetable market in the dramatic play area.
Use oranges as a printing tool for an art activity.

Helpful Hint

Flea markets and garage sales are resources for old juicers.

7.4 Eggs for Breakfast
Scrambled Eggs

Description
Children explore the physical properties of eggs when they crack them open. By using a wire whisk or an eggbeater, they observe physical changes in eggs as they are mixed with air. You assist in cooking the eggs.

Child's Level
This activity is appropriate for older preschool and kindergarten children.

Materials
▲ enough eggs for each child to have one to crack
▲ 1 tablespoon milk per child
▲ inexpensive wire whisk or eggbeater
▲ several small bowls with high sides
▲ hot plate, electric skillet, or microwave

Scientific Information
As children stir the eggs with a whisk or eggbeater, air is mixed with the eggs. A physical change is observable as bubbles form. The parts of the egg mix together, and the color of the new mixture looks different from the original yolk and egg white. When well mixed, the egg mixture cannot be separated back into the original yolk and white. The application of heat causes a chemical change. The scrambled eggs cannot be unscrambled.

Sequence of Implementation
This activity can be implemented in small groups of four or five. You will have more eggs than you need! Each child in the group cracks one egg and adds one tablespoon of milk. All the children can take turns beating the eggs. The teacher will need to cook them. The scrambled eggs can be eaten for breakfast, a snack, or lunch.

What to Look For

Some children may have already had experiences cracking eggs; other children will need assistance.

Children may observe the physical changes in the materials and make comments or ask questions.

Children will beat the eggs enthusiastically.

Questions to Extend Thinking

What is happening to the egg as you beat it?

What happened to the eggs when we heated them?

Do you think the egg will go back to being a liquid again?

Modification

Children may wish to cut up ham or vegetables to add to the eggs in a later cooking activity.

Integrated Curriculum Activities

Use wire whisks and eggbeaters in the sensory table (activity 4.17).

Plan other cooking activities using whisks and eggbeaters, such as making pudding.

Helpful Hint

Search odd-lot stores for inexpensive eggbeaters.

7.5 Baking Shapes
Soft Pretzels

Soft Pretzel Recipe

2 teaspoons dry yeast
¾ cup hot water (at least 105 degrees)

2 teaspoons sugar
2 cups flour

In a large bowl, dissolve the yeast in water. Stir in the sugar. Add the flour. Divide the dough into equal parts, knead, and form shapes. Place the shapes on an ungreased cookie sheet and bake at 325 degrees for 15 minutes. Let cool.

Description

The process of making dough for soft pretzels involves measuring dry and wet ingredients, combining them, and observing the changes. Finally, the mixture is molded by the children who knead, push, poke, and pull the dough. They may appreciate an extended period of time to experiment with many shapes before the teacher bakes the pretzels.

Child's Level

This activity is appropriate for preschool and kindergarten children.

Materials

▲ ingredients for the soft pretzel recipe, which make enough dough for four or five children
▲ toaster oven, if available, or regular oven

Scientific Information

Physical changes occur when dry and wet ingredients are mixed together. The new mixture is different in appearance from the original ingredients and cannot be separated into the original components. The reaction of the sugar and yeast causes bubbles to form and the dough to rise. After cooking, the dough is changed in color and smell. It is no longer sticky and has a fixed shape.

Sequence of Implementation
Making soft pretzels is a simple cooking experience. Both the preparation and baking times are short. Each batch of dough is prepared by a small group of four or five children. Children take turns adding the ingredients and the dough is evenly divided among the group. Each child kneads and shapes the dough before the teacher cooks it.

What to Look For
Many children will manipulate the dough like playdough.
Children may want to taste the raw dough.
Most children will not be able to form the traditional pretzel shape.
Some children will experiment until they form the traditional pretzel shape.

Questions to Extend Thinking
What is happening to the yeast after the sugar is added?
What happened to the pretzels after they baked?
How do you think the pretzels will feel after we bake them?
How does the dough feel when you squeeze it?

Integrated Curriculum Activities
Plan a bakery for the dramatic play area and include multi-cultural play bread and pretzels, if possible.
Use pretzel shapes in a counting song. See *More Than Counting,* by Sally Moomaw and Brenda Hieronymus, activity 2.25.
Read the book *Bread, Bread, Bread,* by Ann Morris.

Helpful Hint
Have some commercial pretzels available for comparison to the soft pretzels.

7.6 Ice Cream in a Can
Effects of Freezing

Ice Cream Recipe

1 cup half-and-half
½ cup sugar
1 teaspoon vanilla
2 pounds ice

2-pound bag of rock salt
1-pound can with lid
3-pound can

In a large bowl, mix together the half-and-half, sugar, and vanilla. Fill the 1-pound can with the mixture only two-thirds of the way to allow for expansion. Seal it with a lid. Place the small can inside the 3-pound can. Chip the ice and layer it with rock salt around the small can (4 parts ice to 1 part salt). Seal the large can.

Roll the cans back and forth on a hard, flat surface. After about ten minutes, open the large can and pour off the water. Carefully open the small can and scrape the ice cream from the sides of the can. Reseal the small can, add more ice and salt, and repeat the process until the ice cream is formed.

Description
This unusual activity allows children to participate fully in all aspects of ice cream making—mixing the cream base, chipping the ice, and making an ice-cream freezer from the 1- and 3-pound cans.

Child's Level
This activity is appropriate for older preschool and kindergarten children.

Materials
For each recipe you will need:

▲ ingredients for the ice cream recipe
▲ gloves or mittens to wear while rolling the cans
▲ wooden mallets to crush the ice cubes

Scientific Information
Water freezes at 32 degrees Fahrenheit. Salt water freezes at a lower temperature. This is why the ocean does not freeze, except at the poles. In this recipe, rock salt is added to the ice to make a mixture that is colder than 32 degrees. This helps speed the process of freezing the ice-cream base in the can. The combination of the lowered temperature and movement of the ice around the raw ingredients inside the small can cause a physical change

in the mixture inside, which produces "iced cream." Since the cold salt water and ice mixture is moving around all surfaces of the can, it helps transfer the heat out of the ice cream mixture, which causes it to freeze.

Sequence of Implementation

1. The first time you make this, have the raw ingredients for the ice cream prepared ahead of time. Set up an area for children to crack the ice into smaller pieces with a wooden mallet or cylinder block. In another area, pairs of children roll the cans back and forth. The process takes a long time, and children will get cold hands. A flat, hard surface is needed for rolling the cans. The process does not work well on carpet or other surfaces. Talk about what is happening on the outside of the can as frost begins to form.
2. In subsequent experiences, the children can mix the ingredients for the cream base before beginning the freezing process.
3. Older children can experiment making the ice cream using ice alone and ice combined with rock salt.

What to Look For

Children will enjoy rolling the can back and forth.

Some children will notice the frost forming on the cans and make comments about their observations.

Children's hands, even wearing mittens or gloves, will get cold from the process.

Children will notice the changes that occur as the ingredients mix and freeze.

Questions to Extend Thinking

What happened to the cream in the can?

Why do you think we need ice?

What is happening on the outside of the can?

Does this ice cream look like the kind you buy at the store?

Integrated Curriculum Activities

Compare the taste of your homemade ice cream to commercial ice milk, ice cream, or frozen yogurt.

Set up an ice-cream store in the dramatic play area.

Helpful Hint

Wrap the ice cubes in old towels when the children crush them.

7.7 Shake, Shake, Shake
Making Butter

Description
Making butter is a familiar activity to many teachers. The children shake small jars of heavy cream until it comes together to form soft butter. Typically the butter is spread on crackers and eaten.

Child's Level
This activity is appropriate for preschool and kindergarten children.

Materials
▲ small plastic or glass jars
▲ heavy whipping cream

Scientific Information
Air inside the jar mixes with the cream to solidify the milk fat, producing what we call butter. This homemade butter differs from some commercial butter since it is soft and does not have salt or coloring added.

Sequence of Implementation
Provide enough jars of cream for children to work together in small groups. Fill each jar half full to allow for the air to mix with the cream. Keep the jar moving from one child to the next by singing the song in this activity. You can add salt to some jars of butter and food coloring to others. Let children taste the samples and make comparisons.

What to Look For
Some children will become engrossed in the process of shaking but not focus on the changes that occur.
Some children will notice the change in the cream and become very excited. There may be some heated discussions among older children about what is happening.
Some children get tired of shaking the jars. Singing the song helps hold their interest.

Diane Blackburn
Used by permission

Shake, shake, shake, make it but-ter, Mix that cream and air.
Shake, shake, shake, make it but-ter, Pass it o - ver there.

Questions to Extend Thinking

What do you think will happen when we shake the cream?

How does the cream look now?

Does this taste like the butter from the store?

Do you think you could make butter by stirring the cream for a
long time?

Modification

Kindergarten children might enjoy planning other shaking activities. They can be quite creative. They might also want to try shaking half-and-half, skim milk, whole milk, soy milk, or other liquids to observe the results.

Integrated Curriculum Activities

Make bread with the children and use the butter to spread on it.

Graph the results of a taste test of margarine, salted butter, light
butter, etc.

Helpful Hint

Take the cream and jars out of the refrigerator for a short period
of time before you begin. This speeds up the process.

7.8 Crack and Grind
Making Peanut Butter

Description
In this activity, children can follow the process of removing peanuts from their shells and transforming them into peanut butter. This can be a two-day process if you use a meat grinder to grind the peanuts, but it can be done in one day if a blender is used. Half of the fun in this activity is cracking open the peanuts and, of course, tasting them. The children experiment with methods of opening peanuts until they find one that works best. The peanuts must be separated from both the outside shells and the thin papery covering on each nut. Some peanuts must be discarded if they appear shriveled or blackened. All of this is fun. The shelled peanuts are placed into a blender or grinder and processed.

Child's Level
This activity is appropriate for preschool children (for whom choking on nuts is not a concern) and for kindergarten children.

Materials
- ▲ one pound of peanuts in the shell for every eight children
- ▲ have an extra bag of shelled peanuts available (in case the children eat too many of the nuts they shell)
- ▲ an old-fashioned meat grinder (or a blender, if time is limited or a grinder is unavailable)
- ▲ peanut oil or vegetable oil to add to the ground nuts for a creamier texture

Scientific Information
Physical characteristics of peanuts that are readily noticed by children include color, size, shape, and a shell that can be cracked open. The peanuts change as they are crushed in the grinder or blender. The addition of oil changes the consistency of the ground peanuts from chunky to creamy.

Sequence of Implementation

Set up this activity for small group participation at one table. Children can rotate through more than once if they choose. Very little supervision is needed except to prevent them from eating the ingredients! This is why you need so many peanuts. Encourage the children to separate the nuts from the shells. Talk about the properties of the shells and nuts. Either grind the nuts in a blender with some oil or save them for the next day to use in the grinder. If you use the grinder, secure it to the table and have children turn the handle and observe the results. If you use the blender, you will be in control of the movement, but children can easily observe the changes through the clear container. Plan to serve the peanut butter for a snack or lunch.

What to Look For

Children will spend a long time opening the peanuts.

Some children will have difficulty opening the peanuts.

Some children will devise unique ways to open the nuts. They may use fingers and fists, or they may get a block or other hard implement to try to crack the shells. This is a good example of the child thinking like a scientist.

Children will be fascinated by the tube-like pieces of peanut butter that emerge through the holes in the grinder. Be prepared for squeals of delight.

Questions to Extend Thinking

What do you think is inside the shell?

What is happening to the peanuts?

Could you make peanut butter just by squeezing the nuts with your fingers? Shaking them in a jar? Pounding them with a hammer?

Integrated Curriculum Activities

Include the book *Nuts to You!*, by Lois Ehlert, in the book area.

Use the meat grinder with playdough (activity 5.21).

Make other kinds of nut butter, such as almond butter.

Helpful Hint

Garage sales and flea markets are good sources for meat grinders.

7.9 Straining Fruit
Making Baby Food

Description
Using a food mill to make strained fruit is easier for children than smashing fruit with a fork. They put whole pieces of fruit into the food mill and turn a crank. The blade pushes the food through the holes in the strainer and into the pan. It emerges in a crushed form that does not look like the original fruit.

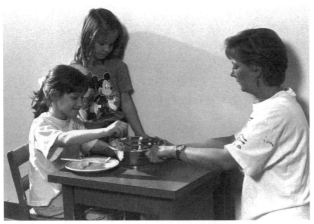

Child's Level
This activity is appropriate for preschool and kindergarten children.

Materials
- ▲ food mill
- ▲ varieties of fruits, such as apples, pears, and bananas
- ▲ small plastic knives
- ▲ tasting spoons

Scientific Information
The fruit changes from whole to part and then into a more liquid state as it is strained. The texture, color, and sometimes the taste change.

Sequence of Implementation
Plan to make two or three varieties of baby food at a time for ease of comparison. The children first cut sections of the fruit into smaller chunks. The chunks are crushed and strained as the child turns the crank on the food mill. Save some examples of the whole fruits, as well as the pieces, for children to observe and compare to the strained fruits. Allow children to taste the fruits before and after they are strained.

What to Look For

Children may have some difficulty holding the food mill while turning the crank.

Some children will turn the crank for only a few rotations, and some will stay with the activity for an extended period.

Children will keep checking the progress of the straining process.

Children may compare the original fruit to the strained fruit.

Children will taste the baby food and make comparisons to whole fruits. Have some processed baby foods available for comparison as well.

Questions to Extend Thinking

What happens when you turn the crank?

Which fruit is the easiest to crush?

What happened to the fruit?

Integrated Curriculum Activities

Ask an interested parent to visit with a baby and let the children watch the baby being fed.

Have the children vote for their favorite baby food and graph the results.

Set up a baby area in the dramatic play area.

Helpful Hint

For easy cleanup, use craft sticks as the tasting spoons.

7.10 Fruit Smoothies
Blending Fruit Shakes

Fruit Smoothies Recipe

¼ banana
3 strawberries
2 tablespoons juice (orange,
   pineapple, etc.)

2 tablespoons yogurt
ice cubes

Put all the ingredients into a blender. Add several ice cubes
and mix.

Description
Children enjoy converting fruits into a snack treat. Since the
fruits in this recipe are soft, a plastic knife can be used to cut
them. Children observe changes in the fruits as they cut them and
as the fruits are processed in a blender.

Child's Level
This activity is appropriate for preschool
and kindergarten children.

Materials
▲ ingredients for the fruit smoothies
   recipe
▲ small plastic knives
▲ a blender

Scientific Information
The physical properties of fruits include
color, shape, texture, and taste, which all
change during the process of cutting and
blending. Once the ingredients are blended, they cannot be separated into the original components again. The addition of ice
causes a change in the fruit and yogurt from cool to very cold.
The ice changes from a solid to a liquid form.

Sequence of Implementation

Set up this activity in stations so that children will not have to wait too long. After several children complete the steps listed below, they can drink the fruit smoothie.

1. At the first station, children cut the fruit.
2. At the second station, children measure and add the yogurt.
3. At the final station, the teacher adds the ice cubes and operates the blender. The fruit drink can be poured into cups and served at snack time.

What to Look For

Children will easily cut the soft fruits with the plastic knife.

Children will observe and make comments about the physical properties of the different fruits. Some may communicate these observations to others.

Many children will want to taste the fruits they cut. You may start the cooking activity by tasting each of the fruits and then re-direct children away from further tasting until the activity is complete.

Some children will participate in the activity but not taste the drink.

Questions to Extend Thinking

Can you see any of the pieces of fruit in the drink after it is blended?

What happened to the banana?

Do you taste the banana (strawberry, yogurt) in the fruit smoothie?

Integrated Curriculum Activities

Plan to make fruit salad with some of the same fruits.

Plan a fruit and vegetable market in the dramatic play area. Include plastic fruits and vegetables.

Take a field trip to a grocery store or local fruit market to purchase the ingredients.

Use plastic knives with playdough.

Read *Eating the Alphabet,* by Lois Ehlert.

Helpful Hint

Send a copy of the recipe home for parents.

Science in Gross-Motor Areas

Dani approached the empty teeter-totter and sat on the down side. She waited about thirty seconds and then said, "Hey, this thing's broken!" She had just begun a series of explorations of the lever and fulcrum.

▲ ▲ ▲

Adrienne and Cate stacked empty salt boxes. They used a bean-bag to knock over the target. Cate was successful in her attempt, but Adrienne was not. Adrienne moved closer to the target and tried again. This time she was successful! Her decision to move closer was a result of her observations of her actions and the reactions of the boxes.

▲ ▲ ▲

Gross-motor play is a naturally occurring event in the lives of children and a common part of the curriculum in early childhood programs. You may remember your own childhood experiences and the anticipation of outdoor activities. Did you know then that you were participating in scientific explorations? Probably not. However, explorations in the gross-motor areas provide many opportunities for children to apply scientific principles and construct relationships about the physical properties of objects and the results of actions on objects. They encounter problems to solve and use elements of the scientific process to find solutions. Children spend extended periods of time trying out solutions as they vary actions, objects, distance, and weight, for example. These explorations help lay a foundation for a more abstract understanding of physics in the future.

Teachers' Questions

What gross-motor activities promote the scientific process?

Activities that involve the movement of objects present interesting problems for children to solve. As they ponder the solutions to problems in the gross-motor areas, they must consider their own actions in relationship to the reactions of the materials. This often leads to *disequilibrium*—a lack of balance between what children think and what children observe. Disequilibrium generally motivates children to search for higher-level understanding. For example, based on their experiences, children typically expect round objects to roll. This information might lead the teacher to plan a game in which children knock over a stack of cardboard blocks by rolling a ball. Later, a ball-shaped beanbag might be substituted for the ball. The new ball, however, does not respond as the children have come to expect of round objects. Some children are so bothered by the unexpected behavior of the beanbag ball that they refuse to use it. Other children, though also bothered, persist in trying to use the new beanbag ball. These children are in disequilibrium and are motivated to continue to seek more information about round things.

What types of gross-motor activities involve the movement of objects?

Gross-motor activities in which children use their bodies to manipulate objects encourage the construction of scientific information about the movement of objects. For example, children may throw, kick, pull, or roll objects such as balls, beanbags, ropes, and other materials. In doing so, they learn about how their actions affect the reactions of these objects. The activities in this chapter use many common pieces of gross-motor equipment in some familiar and not so familiar ways. Children experiment with how to knock over objects, aim for a target, or catch a rolling object. They may use one object to affect another object, or they may employ simple machines or pendulums to experiment with objects.

What types of gross-motor activities involve simple machines?

Activities that involve pulleys, inclined planes, or levers can be designed for the gross-motor areas. As children lift objects to the top of the climber with a pulley, roll objects down the slide (inclined plane) to hit a target, or attempt to balance on the teeter-totter (lever), they gather important scientific knowledge through the use of their whole body in relationship to these simple machines. Since cognitive development cannot be separated from physical development, gross-motor experiences with simple machines are an excellent vehicle for learning.

What types of gross-motor activities involve pendulums?

Pendulums can be used to knock over targets or to observe the elliptical patterns created by their movements. Children can adjust their actions when using pendulums to solve problems created by the activities. Through observing the results of their actions and making alterations, children construct knowledge about the pendulum.

Why is it important for teachers to integrate science activities into the gross-motor curriculum?

Gross-motor play allows children to use their whole bodies to experience the physical properties of materials. Scientific learning is a natural outgrowth of children's explorations of materials, equipment, and their bodies in space. Teachers can maximize the opportunities for the construction of scientific knowledge in the indoor and outdoor play areas.

All early childhood programs plan daily outdoor experiences for children. Many programs also have an indoor space designed for gross-motor activity. In these areas children explore the physical properties of objects, as well as create relationships between actions and reactions. Some of the activities for the gross-motor areas are similar or related to activities found in chapter 3, "Machines and Pendulums."

What scientific principles emerge as children experiment with gross-motor equipment and activities?

Gross-motor activities encourage children to explore the physical properties of materials as well as the relationships between their actions and the reactions of the materials. The resulting construction of physical knowledge enables children to lay a foundation for the later abstract study of physics. These activities encourage children who might otherwise avoid science to explore the movement of objects, an important scientific process. Children also experiment with directed force, as in target games, and the use of tools or machines, such as pulleys.

What relationships can children create through explorations with gross-motor equipment and materials?

Children create many relationships between their actions on objects and the reactions of those objects. They observe how objects respond to the effects of changes in weight, height, distance, balance, and force applied to them. Information about specific relationships is identified for each activity in this chapter.

How can teachers better use gross-motor activity books to promote science?

Teachers can select activities that encourage children to create relationships between their actions on objects and the reactions of the gross-motor equipment. Activity books for indoor and outdoor play typically focus on the development of muscle strength and skill, cooperation with others, or organized games with rules. They do not address the scientific potential embedded in the activities. Therefore, teachers must plan additions to the equipment, sequence the activities, and include variations to help children focus on particular scientific principles.

What gross-motor equipment and materials are needed to encourage scientific thinking?

Many standard pieces of gross-motor equipment, such as climbers and slides, teeter-totters, ladders, or sawhorses and planks, can be designed to encourage scientific explorations. These materials are already an important part of many early childhood programs. Accessories such as balls, beanbags, tubes, and empty bottles may be used in the outdoor and indoor areas. These and other teacher-developed materials are included in the activities in this chapter.

Where can teachers find the additional equipment needed to enhance the possibilities for scientific learning in the gross-motor areas?

Some of the equipment can be purchased through catalogs, but many of the accessories are assembled from free or inexpensive resources. In many instances, teachers combine existing equipment to create the potential for scientific learning. In other instances, the equipment and accessories are made by teachers and parent volunteers. You will find specific instructions for how to combine equipment or make the accessories for each activity in this chapter.

How do teachers organize and set up gross-motor areas to maximize the potential for scientific learning in these areas?

Teachers plan and set up the equipment in the indoor or outdoor environment to highlight specific scientific principles. The areas remain the same for an extended period of time so children can become deeply involved in the exploration of the scientific concepts inherent in the design. Teachers have long-range as well as short-term goals in mind. For example, teachers might introduce a ramp activity in the gross-motor room because children have been interested in a small ramp-bowling game in the classroom. However, once introduced, teachers might follow a long-term sequence of ramp activities so that children could more fully explore the properties of ramps. Varying the height and length of the ramp, changing the objects to roll down it, altering the surface of the ramp, and planning where children roll things up the ramp are some of the long-range possibilities. While teachers will, of course, be limited by the equipment that exists at their schools, they can adapt the ideas presented to fit the needs of their programs.

How do teachers sequence the activities in the gross-motor areas?

Teachers begin with a simple version of an activity. The activity increases in complexity through minor changes or additions to the activity. For example, when children are exploring balls, teachers might start with large plastic balls, which are familiar to young children. Later, balls with unusual surfaces, such as sponge or cloth, might be introduced. Eventually, weighted balls could be included. They respond very differently from typical balls and cause children to ponder the reasons for this, based on their earlier experiences with balls. Specific information about sequencing can be found in the activities in this chapter.

What is the teacher's role?

The teacher creates gross-motor areas rich in potential for scientific learning, makes additions or changes to increase the complexity of the activity, and asks well-timed questions to encourage thinking and further cognitive development. Teachers encourage children to actively experiment with the materials and reflect on the results. More information about explorations of the movement of objects and questions to stimulate thinking can be found in chapter 3, "Machines and Pendulums."

How can teachers assess children's understanding of scientific principles in gross-motor areas?

Teachers can record information on an assessment form, such as the one included in appendix A.10. In many early childhood programs, teachers may share the gross-motor areas with other groups. The class assessment form (appendix A.11) provides a method for teachers or volunteers to record information about children from other classrooms.

Gross-Motor
Activities

8.1 Can You Catch It?
Incline

Description
The physical properties of objects affect how they roll down an incline. In this activity, children experiment with a variety of objects on a ramp in a gross-motor area. Make the structure (pictured below) out of hollow wooden blocks, of which nine are rectangular blocks and two are ramp blocks. If hollow blocks are not available, try to modify an existing slide to accomplish the same result. Stack the rectangular blocks in three sections of four, three, and two blocks. Place a ramp block on top of each stack to make one continuous slope.

Child's Level
This activity is appropriate for older preschool and kindergarten children.

Materials
- ▲ hollow blocks, as pictured
- ▲ hard cardboard tubes, balls, or other objects that roll
- ▲ a large box to place at the lowest end of the ramp
- ▲ small boxes or saucepans for catching objects at the end of the ramp

Scientific Information
The placement of the object at the top of the ramp and the angle at which it is rolled affect its position at the bottom of the ramp.

Sequence of Implementation
1. Begin this activity with cardboard tubes so that children will focus on rolling objects. If you begin with balls, children will probably want to play with them in a way that is familiar — throwing and catching. Place the large box at the end of the ramp to encourage children to aim and to help contain the rolling objects.
2. After one week of exploration, offer some other objects that roll, such as smaller tubes or wooden dowels.
3. After two weeks, include the small boxes or saucepans so that children can try to catch the objects before they fall off of the ramp.

What to Look For
Children may try to take apart the structure to play with the
blocks. Redirect them to other activities or engage them in the
ramp activity.
Children will be very excited when the tubes fly off the end.
Some children will race the tubes down the ramp.
Other children will adjust the large box in order to catch the
tubes.
Several children may cooperate in rolling and catching the tubes.

Comments and Questions to Extend Thinking
What can you do to roll the tube into the box?
Where will you hold the saucepan to catch the ball?
I wonder why that one keeps rolling off the side.

Modification
Add or subtract blocks to change the height of the ramp.

Integrated Curriculum Activities
Include other ramp activities in the classroom (activities 3.1, 3.2,
3.3, 5.7, 5.8, and 8.2).
Make a ramp outside for tricycles.

Helpful Hint
If children ignore the activity, try rolling a few tubes and ask
some children to try to catch them. This may generate some
interest and get things started.

8.2 Aim for the Can
Incline

Description
This activity uses the same blocks and design as activity 8.1, but with some slight alterations. Children roll the balls up the ramp rather than down. The ramp is wider and the height of the structure is lower to offer children more control when aiming for a specific target. Place three of the rectangular blocks side by side and place one ramp block on top of each. Use duct tape to secure the ramp block to the rectangular block and to secure the three sections together. You can also make a ramp from a piece of plywood supported by boxes.

Child's Level
This activity is appropriate for older preschool and kindergarten children.

Materials
- ▲ hollow blocks, as pictured
- ▲ three 3-pound cans covered with contact paper
- ▲ tennis balls or other small balls about 3 inches in diameter

Scientific Information
When an object is rolled up a slope, the force of gravity acts to pull it down the slope. If the object has enough speed to counteract gravity, it will reach the top; otherwise, it will roll partway up the slope, stop momentarily, and then roll back to the bottom.

Sequence of Implementation
1. Plan this activity after other ramp activities in which children roll objects down a slope.
2. Begin with one type of ball to give children time to construct information about the ramp without any other variables to consider.
3. Add slightly different balls, such as a racquetball.
4. Include a score sheet and pencils for children who are interested.

What to Look For
Rolling objects up a slope is more challenging than rolling them down.

Some children will roll the ball from the midpoint of the ramp.

Some children will ignore the ramp and drop the balls into the cans.

Many children will roll objects down the ramp as they have in other ramp activities.

Children will attempt to roll the balls up the ramp and get them into the cans.

Some children will quantify how many balls land in the cans.

Questions to Extend Thinking
Where do you start rolling the ball to make it go in this can?

What can you do to keep the ball from rolling back to you?

If you sit here and roll the ball, can you make it go here?

Modifications
Change the objects that are rolled up the ramp.

Cover the cans with different colors of contact paper so that children can aim for a specific can and keep score, if desired.

Integrated Curriculum Activities
Plan other ramp activities in the classroom (activities 3.1, 3.2, 3.3, 5.7, 5.8, and 8.1).

Include a ramp for tricycles in the outside area.

Helpful Hint
Try substituting a toddler slide for the ramp if you cannot build one.

8.3 Send It Over, Please
Horizontal Pulley

Description
The horizontal pulley system allows children to experiment with moving objects without having to walk. This pulley system is made using a horizontal ladder frame turned upside down. You can also use a commercial pulley frame or mount the pulleys on other pieces of equipment, such as one on a climber and one on a wall. The pulleys are attached to each end of the ladder frame by tying them to one of the rungs. A basket is secured to the rope using duct tape.

Child's Level
This activity is appropriate for preschool and kindergarten children.

Materials
▲ pulley system, as described above
▲ small objects to send across the pulley system, such as rubber farm animals or plastic fruits and vegetables

Scientific Information
Pulleys allow us to change the direction of moving objects without changing our position. Pulling the rope in one direction moves the basket in the opposite direction. (See page 52 for a description of pulleys.)

Sequence of Implementation
1. Place a small box or basket at each end of the pulley system. Include a selection of small objects for children to send back and forth.
2. During the second week, change the materials available to send across the pulley system.

What to Look For

Many children will pull the rope in the direction they want the object to move and be surprised when it moves the opposite way.

Children may walk over to the basket and move it toward the other person.

Children will figure out where to pull the rope to move it in the direction they choose to send the objects.

Some children who are watching may help solve the problem of how to move the objects accurately. It may be easier for them to observe the movement of the basket since they can view the whole system at once.

Questions to Extend Thinking

How can you move the basket?

Which rope do you pull to make the basket move toward you?

What do you have to do to move the objects to Connie?

Modification

Place two pulley systems side by side for comparison.

Integrated Curriculum Activities

Plan other pulley activities in the science area (activities 3.13 and 3.14).

Suspend a pulley system over the water table for drying doll clothes (activity 4.16).

Helpful Hint

Pulleys can be purchased at many hardware stores.

8.4 Send It Up, Please
Vertical Pulley

Description
In this activity, children explore the movement of objects both up to and down from the platform of a climber. Attach a pulley to the top of the climber with rope, and attach a bucket to the other end. Fashion a handle at the top by forming a loop of rope and wrapping colored tape around it. Children can send objects up and down to each other using the pulley.

Child's Level
This activity is appropriate for preschool and kindergarten children.

Materials
- ▲ a climbing frame, as pictured, or suspend the pulley from the ceiling
- ▲ a large pulley, attached to the climber with rope, with a bucket at the bottom of the pulley rope
- ▲ beanbags or other soft objects
- ▲ objects such as toy farm animals or plastic fruits and vegetables

Scientific Information
A pulley makes the work of moving objects easier. Pulling down to lift things is easier than pulling up. A pulley makes this possible.

Sequence of Implementation
1. Begin with beanbags or other soft objects so that children focus on the pulley rather than playing with the objects.
2. Change to other objects for lifting.
3. Change to heavier objects for comparison to other experiences.

What to Look For
Some children will use their hands to lift the bucket attached to the rope.

Many children will figure out how to lift the bucket by pulling down on the rope.

Children will experiment with lifting and lowering objects by using the pulley.

Questions to Extend Thinking
How can you move this bucket to the top of the climber without carrying it up?
What happens if you pull on the handle of the rope?

Modification
Add a horizontal pulley to the climber so that children can move objects up and across the climber.

Integrated Curriculum Activities
Include other pulley activities in the classroom (activities 3.13, 5.9, and 8.3).
Suspend a vertical pulley over the sandbox for lifting sand.

Helpful Hint
Tie a bead to the pulley rope to keep the bucket from slamming to the floor when children let go of it. Attach the bucket to one end of the rope, thread it through the pulley, attach the bead on the other side, and then form the handle.

8.5 Knock It Down
Pendulum Target

Description
This activity is a larger version of activity 3.17, "Wrecking Ball." Make the pendulum shown by suspending a weight from the A-frame of a tire swing. You can suspend a pendulum from the ceiling as well. Children can discover the properties of the pendulum as they try to knock over plastic bottles. They can also explore the effects of the type of target, the weight and height of the target, the weight of the pendulum, and the length of the rope attached to the pendulum.

Child's Level
This activity is appropriate for preschool and kindergarten children.

Materials
▲ pendulum frame, as shown
▲ a length of rope attached to a plastic jar filled with rocks
▲ 1- or 2-liter plastic bottles

Scientific Information
The pendulum moves in an arc-shaped path. The distance it can swing depends on the length of the rope attached to the weight. The weight of the pendulum affects the ease of knocking over the target. The weight of the target affects the ability of the pendulum to knock it over.

Sequence of Implementation
1. Begin with four or five empty bottles for the target. This ensures that the pendulum will knock them over if it hits them.
2. Measure the length of rope attached to the pendulum to ensure that it is long enough so that the pendulum can hit the bottles.
3. Set up the target when children are not using the pendulum. This gives them some opportunities to view it and perhaps helps them figure out how to do it themselves.
4. After an extended period of time for exploration, change the weight of the target bottles by adding water or sand.
5. Other changes can be made once children have become adept at knocking over the bottles. Change the length of the rope, or change the weight of the pendulum by filling the jar with lighter weight material.

What to Look For

Many children view the pendulum like a ball and attempt to throw it at the target bottles.

Children require a substantial period of experimentation to figure out how to place the target so that the pendulum can reach it.

Some children will cooperate to solve the problems of target placement or how to release the pendulum.

Some children will quantify how many bottles they knock over.

Questions to Extend Thinking

How can you knock over these bottles?

I notice that the pendulum didn't hit any bottles. Is there another way to set up the bottles?

What happens if you release the pendulum and watch it swing?

Modification

Substitute thick cardboard tubes for the bottles. They can be stacked. This may help children notice where the pendulum swings.

Integrated Curriculum Activities

Plan a painting activity that uses a pendulum (activity 5.11).

Include the book *Machines at Work,* by Byron Barton, in the reading area.

Helpful Hint

Place a metal washer inside the jar lid to prevent the knot on the rope from slipping through the hole in the lid.

8.6 Draw An Ellipse
Tire Swing Pendulum

Description
This activity may help children observe the arc-shaped path of a pendulum. The child holds a marker and lies face down on the tire swing. A large piece of butcher paper is on the floor under the tire swing. The teacher or another child gives the tire a push and the child places the marker on the paper. As the tire swing moves, the marker traces the path it makes.

Child's Level
This activity is appropriate for kindergarten children.

Materials
▲ tire swing
▲ marker and large sheets of butcher paper

Scientific Information
The pendulum moves in an arc-shaped or elliptical path.

Sequence of Implementation
1. Begin by having the child hold one marker.
2. Give the child a different colored marker for each hand.

What to Look For
This will be very exciting! Be prepared for a long waiting list.
Some children may not be able to balance and keep the marker on the paper at all times during the process.
The tire swing may not rotate long enough for the elliptical path to become apparent.

Questions to Extend Thinking
What do you think will happen when Kim holds the marker on the paper as the swing moves?
Do you think Reina will make a bigger track or a smaller track as the pendulum slows down?

Modification
Place a small swimming pool under the tire swing. Fill the pool with a shallow layer of sand. Let the children use their fingers to make the track in the sand.

Integrated Curriculum Activities
Include other pendulum activities in the classroom (activities 3.17, 3.18, and 3.19).
Plan a construction site in the dramatic play area. Construction sites often include a wrecking ball, which is a pendulum.

Helpful Hint
You may need to push the swing in order to give it enough momentum.

8.7 Knock It Down
Bowling

Description
In this activity, children roll a variety of balls to knock over a target made of plastic bottles.

Child's Level
This activity is appropriate for preschool and kindergarten children.

Materials
- ▲ a variety of sizes of balls, such as a large plastic ball, tennis ball, basketball, and a ball with a weight inside
- ▲ eight or more plastic bottles, such as 1-liter or shampoo bottles

Scientific Information
The size or weight of a ball and the force applied to the ball affect one's ability to knock over a target, such as bottles. Standing closer to the target may make it easier for children to knock over the bottles.

Sequence of Implementation
1. Begin with eight empty bottles and the large plastic ball. Children can practice setting up the bottles and knocking them over. It will take some experimenting for them to construct how to place the bottles in a group in order to knock over several at once.
2. After one week, introduce a different ball, such as the tennis ball or a basketball.
3. Later, change the type of bottles used, or change the weight by adding sand or water.
4. After an extended period of exploration by children, change to the ball with a weight inside. It will respond in unexpected ways.

What to Look For

Children may want to play with the balls. Redirect them to the bowling game with a question such as, "How can you knock over the bottles with that ball?"

Children may cooperate to make the target and take turns rolling the ball.

Some children may need assistance creating a target with the bottles.

Children may experiment and figure out the best way to set up the bottles and knock down the most with one roll of the ball.

Some children may keep score as they knock down the bottles.

Questions to Extend Thinking

How can you knock over these bottles with the ball?
Where would you aim to knock over this one?
Which ball do you think will knock over the most bottles?

Modification

Add score sheets and pencils for children who may want to keep score.

Integrated Curriculum Activities

Plan other target games (activity 8.8).
Design a small bowling game for the science area of the classroom. Film canisters make good bowling pins.

Helpful Hint

Create a special space for the bowling game in the gross-motor areas. You can use masking tape or colored tape to enclose the space and hang up a sign that says *Knock down the bottles*.

8.8 Stack It Up
Beanbag Target Game

Description
Children create a target by stacking empty salt boxes and use a beanbag to knock over the target.

Child's Level
This activity is appropriate for older preschool and kindergarten children.

Materials
▲ eight or more empty salt boxes attractively painted or covered with contact paper
▲ beanbags and teacher-made bags filled with Styrofoam or other lightweight substances

Scientific Information
The physical properties of the salt boxes affect how they must be stacked in order to balance. The type of beanbag and distance from the target affect the children's ability to knock over the boxes. The way the boxes are stacked influences how many are knocked over at the same time.

Sequence of Implementation
1. Begin with commercial or teacher-made beanbags and six to eight empty salt boxes.
2. Introduce several more salt boxes.
3. Add the teacher-made bags filled with Styrofoam.

What to Look For
Children may line up the boxes horizontally to knock them over.
Some children will figure out how to stack the boxes vertically and knock them over.
Some children will experiment and discover how to knock over the boxes using the lightweight bags.
Children will adjust how they stack the boxes and how far they stand from the target and discover how to best knock over the boxes.

Questions to Extend Thinking
What happens if you stack some of the boxes on top of each other and then throw the beanbag?
If you stand here will you be able to knock over more boxes?
Is it easier to knock over the boxes with the beanbag or with the other bag?
How would you stack the boxes if you wanted to knock over all of them at the same time?
Where did you hit the stack of boxes to knock over so many?

Modification
Change to full salt boxes or other weighted boxes.

Integrated Curriculum Activities
Plan other target games, such as activity 8.7.
Use the salt boxes with the pendulum game (activity 8.5).

Helpful Hint
Ask parents to save salt boxes for you.

8.9 Teeter-Totter
Balance

Description
A teeter-totter is a type of lever with the fulcrum in the middle. In this activity, children explore the effects of the movement of objects in a clear plastic tube attached to the teeter-totter. The movement of the objects inside the tube may help them construct information about balance. Instead of placing weights on each side of a balance, the children themselves are the weights.

Child's Level
This activity is appropriate for older preschool and kindergarten children.

Materials
- ▲ a commercial teeter-totter, as pictured
- ▲ 36-inch piece of clear tubing, at least 1 inch in diameter, sealed at both ends
- ▲ small objects such as marbles, beads, and magnetic marbles to place inside the tube before sealing the ends
- ▲ clear tape for securing the tube to the teeter-totter

Scientific Information
Gravity pulls the heavier side of the teeter-totter more than the lighter side, which causes the heavier side to go down. As children push on the floor, they create an upward force that causes a shift in balance. This causes the down side of the lever to go up. The objects inside the tube always roll to the lower end of the lever as it moves up and down.

Sequence of Implementation
1. Begin by placing a black marble into the tube, sealing the ends, and securing it to the teeter-totter. You may need to redirect children away from removing the tubing from the teeter-totter.
2. Add one or more marbles to the tube and reattach it to the teeter-totter.
3. Wrap pieces of colored tape around several places on the tube. Ask children if they can stop the marble under the tape.
4. Change to magnetic marbles which respond differently than several loose marbles.

What to Look For

Children may use the teeter-totter but ignore the tube and marbles.

Some children will notice the marbles inside the tube and observe the movement.

Some children will try to see how fast they can make the marble move inside the tube.

Children may move the teeter-totter while sitting next to it instead of on it.

Questions to Extend Thinking

What can you do to make the marble move slowly inside the tube?

How can you make the marble stop moving?

What would you do to make the marble stop under the red tape?

Modification

Remove the tube from the teeter-totter and allow children to manipulate it and observe the movement of the marble.

Integrated Curriculum Activities

Include clear tubes, marbles, and corks in the sensory table (activity 4.5).

Include a balance activity in the science area (activity 3.9).

Helpful Hint

The clear tubing can be purchased in aquarium supply stores.

8.10 Tube Tunnels
Inclines

Description
This unique activity uses clear tubing hooked together with dryer-vent hose and duct tape. Children have many opportunities to change the angle or slope of the inclines. They can create one long slope or a zigzag pattern and observe a ball roll along the path.

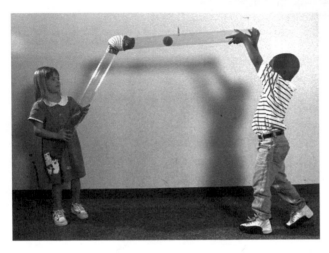

Original design by Nancy Eling.

Child's Level
This activity is most appropriate for older preschool and kindergarten children.

Materials
- ▲ several 3-foot sections of clear plastic tubing, 4 or 5 inches in diameter
- ▲ dryer-vent hose in the corresponding diameter
- ▲ duct tape for attaching the dryer-vent hose to the plastic tubes
- ▲ a variety of balls (tennis balls, jack balls, Ping-Pong balls, and Koosh balls)

Scientific Information
Objects move to the lowest point of the tube or tubes. The angle of the tube affects the speed of movement of the balls.

Sequence of Implementation
1. Begin with one tube with a ball inside and the ends sealed. This is similar to activity 4.5, "Tubing and Corks." Holding and moving one tube is easier than coordinating the movement of several tubes connected together.
2. Vary the type of ball in the tube.
3. Connect two or more tubes together with the duct tape and add the tennis ball. After some exploration by the children, offer a variety of balls.

What to Look For

Children will tip the tube up and down to watch the ball move.

Some children will carefully move the tubing to control the movement of the ball.

Children may cooperate to coordinate the movement of several tubes connected together.

Questions to Extend Thinking

How can you make this ball move inside the tube?

What would you do to make it go through all the tubes and out the end?

LaVonne made the ball move backward. Can you make yours move backward, too?

Modification

Attach smaller or larger diameter tubing together for comparison.

Integrated Curriculum Activities

Attach a clear tube to the teeter-totter (activity 8.9).

Plan sensory table activities using clear tubes (activities 4.5 and 4.6).

Helpful Hint

Look in the phone book for a local plastics company. They may donate a few tubes to your school.

Appendix

A.1 Resource Information

The following list contains information on the books mentioned in *More Than Magnets* that may be useful when trying to locate these resources at libraries or stores.

Chapter One:
Piaget's Theory of Cognitive and Affective Development (4th ed.), by Barry J. Wadsworth (White Plains, NY: Longman, 1989).

Chapter Two:
The Big Tree and The Little Tree, by Mary Augusta Lappage (Winnipeg: Pemmican, 1986).
Bird Nests, by Eileen Curran (Mahwah, NJ: Troll, 1985).
Chicka Chicka Boom Boom, by Bill Martin Jr. and John Archambault (New York: Simon & Schuster, 1989).
Coconut Kind of Day, by Lynn Joseph (New York: Lothrop, 1990).
Digging Up Dinosaurs, by Aliki (New York: Harper, 1981).
Feathers for Lunch, by Lois Ehlert (New York: Harcourt, 1990).
More Than Counting: Whole Math Activities for Preschool and Kindergarten, by Sally Moomaw and Brenda Hieronymus (St. Paul: Redleaf, 1995).
More Than Singing: Discovering Music in Preschool and Kindergarten, by Sally Moomaw (St. Paul: Redleaf, 1997).
Nuts to You!, by Lois Ehlert (New York: Harcourt, 1993).
The Popcorn Book, by Tomie de Paola (New York: Holiday, 1978).
Pumpkin Pumpkin, by Jeanne Titherington (New York: Greenwillow, 1986).
Squirrels, by Brian Wildsmith (New York: Oxford UP, 1974).
Swimmy, by Leo Lionni (New York: Pantheon, 1968).
This Year's Garden, by Cynthia Rylant (New York: Aladdin, 1987).

Chapter Three:
Bam, Bam, Bam, by Eve Merriam (New York: Scholastic, 1994).
Machines at Work, by Byron Barton (New York: Harper, 1987).
More Than Counting: Whole Math Activities for Preschool and Kindergarten, by Sally Moomaw and Brenda Hieronymus (St. Paul: Redleaf, 1995).
More Than Singing: Discovering Music in Preschool and Kindergarten, by Sally Moomaw (St. Paul: Redleaf, 1997).
Pancakes, Pancakes, by Eric Carle (New York: Scholastic, 1990).
Physical Knowledge in Preschool Education, by Constance Kamii and Rheta DeVries (New York: Prentice-Hall, 1978).

The Popcorn Book, by Tomie de Paola (New York: Scholastic, 1978).
Raccoons and Ripe Corn, by Jim Arnosky (New York: Scholastic, 1987).
The Story of the Milky Way, A Cherokee Tale, by Joseph Bruchac and Gayle Ross (New York: Dial, 1995).
The Tortilla Factory, by Gary Paulsen (New York: Harcourt, 1995).
Wish I Had a Big, Big Tree, by Satoru Sato (New York: Lothrop, 1989).

Chapter Four:
The Big Enough Helper, by Nancy Hall (New York: Western, 1978).
Bones, Bones, Dinosaur Bones, by Byron Barton (New York: Crowell, 1990).
Bubble Bubble, by Mercer Mayer (Roxbury, CT: Rain Bird, 1992).
Bubble Festival (GEMS, Lawrence Hall of Science, University of California, Berkeley).
Charlie Needs a Cloak, by Tomie de Paola (New York: Simon & Schuster, 1973).
Digging Up Dinosaurs, by Aliki (New York: Crowell, 1978).
The Doorbell Rang, by Pat Hutchins (New York: Morrow, 1986).
Hammers, Nails, Planks and Paint, by Thomas Campbell Jackson (New York: Scholastic, 1994).
King Bidgood's in the Bathtub, by Audrey Wood (New York: Harcourt, 1986).
More Than Counting: Whole Math Activities for Preschool and Kindergarten, by Sally Moomaw and Brenda Hieronymus (St. Paul: Redleaf, 1995).
The Patchwork Quilt, by Valorie Flourney (New York: Dial, 1985).
Physical Knowledge in Preschool Education, by Constance Kamii and Rheta DeVries (New York: Prentice-Hall, 1978).
Pizza Party, by Grace Maccarone (New York: Scholastic, 1994).
A Pocket for Corduroy, by Don Freeman (New York: Viking, 1968).
Skyscraper Going Up, by Vicki Cobb (New York: Crowell, 1987).
Who Sank the Boat? by Pamela Allen (New York: Coward-McCann, 1982).
Yellow Ball, by Molly Bang (New York: Morrow, 1991).

Chapter Five:
Constructive Play: Applying Piaget in the Preschool, by George Forman and Fleet Hill (Menlo Park, CA: Addison-Wesley, 1984).
Earth Daughter, by Joseph Ancona (New York: Simon & Schuster, 1995).
Feathers for Lunch, by Lois Ehlert (New York: Harcourt, 1990).
It Looked Like Spilt Milk, by Charles G. Shaw (New York: Harper, 1993).
Owl Babies, by Martin Waddel (Cambridge, MA: Candlewick, 1992).
Swimmy, by Leo Lionni (New York: Knopf, 1963).

Chapter Six:
Max Found Two Sticks, by Brian Pinkney (New York: Simon & Schuster, 1994).
Max, the Music-Maker, by Miriam B. Strecher and Alice S. Kandell (New York: Lothrop, 1980).
More Than Counting: Whole Math Activities for Preschool and Kindergarten, by Sally Moomaw and Brenda Hieronymus (St. Paul: Redleaf, 1995).
More Than Singing: Discovering Music in Preschool and Kindergarten, by Sally Moomaw (St. Paul: Redleaf, 1997).

Chapter Seven:
Bread, Bread, Bread, by Ann Morris (New York: Lothrop, 1989).
Eating the Alphabet, by Lois Ehlert (New York: Harcourt, 1989).
Growing Vegetable Soup, by Lois Ehlert (New York: Harcourt, 1987).
Nuts to You!, by Lois Ehlert (New York: Harcourt, 1993).

Chapter Eight:
Machines at Work, by Byron Barton (New York: Harper, 1987).

A.2 Terms and Definitions

TERM	DEFINITION	EXAMPLE
hypothesize	to assume or suppose before experimenting	The child assumes that the weight suspended from the pendulum is thrown like a ball.
predict	to state or suggest the outcome before experimenting	A child predicts which objects will roll all the way down a ramp before trying out the activity.
observe	to examine or study carefully	A child stares at a shell and pokes, smells, and rubs its surface. The child might use the magnifier to more closely attend to details.
compare	to examine two or more objects, actions, or reactions of materials for similarities and differences	A child alternately shakes fresh gourds and dried gourds and places them in two separate baskets based on whether or not a noise is produced by shaking them.
experiment	a process used to explore materials, actions, and reactions of objects	A child strikes a triangle on each side, spins it on the handle, and bangs it against the table in an attempt to find out more about triangles.
classify	to group together by similar attributes	A child suggests that the pretzel dough is like playdough. A child groups together all the shells that have ridges.
infer	to draw a conclusion through reasoning after experimenting	A child concludes that all round objects roll. A child reasons that bigger instruments have a lower pitch.

A.3 Individual Assessment Form for Science Activities

CHILD:

hypothesize	predict	observe	compare	experiment	classify	infer	additional comments

A.4 Class Assessment Form for Science Activities

Science Activity:

Name of Child	hypothesize	predict	observe	compare	experiment	classify	infer	additional comments

A.5 Sample Individual Assessment for Science Displays

Displays	hypothesize	predict	observe	compare	experiment	classify	infer	additional comments
Acorns					9/24 hits two together	9/30 size 10/5 type		
Bird Nests		11/10 "This one has a hundred seeds."	10/22 uses magnifier					10/22 describes parts of nests
Gourds			11/10 "These have stripes."			11/30 color 11/15 shape		
Tops	12/3 "Square ones won't spin."		11/30 watches others spin tops			12/7 spins two at once		

A.6 Sample Individual Assessment for Machines and Pendulums

CHILD: AsA

Displays	hypothesize	predict	observe	compare	experiment	classify	infer	additional comments
Open & Shut (lever)					10/6 uses lid to pry open other lids			
Wrecking Ball (pendulum)		2/27 shorter rope will still knock over bottles	2/12 watches others		2/14 throws harder		2/20 placing bottles close together is easier	
Ramps & Things	4/1 "All round objects will roll."		4/1 some objects do not roll		4/8 raises level of ramp			
Adjustable Ramp	4/15 "The higher the ramp, the faster things roll."			4/12 wheels and balls	4/13 lifts ramp while balls roll	4/10 sorts spheres from other objects		

A.7 Sample Individual Assessment for Science in the Sensory Table

CHILD: EMILY

Activities	hypothesize	predict	observe	compare	experiment	classify	infer	additional comments
Funnels (with dry materials)			10/5 beans won't go through hole	12/1 rice and beans	12/1 stops flow with hand			
Colanders (with rice)			3/6 many holes				3/7 similar to funnels	
Tubes/Corks (with water)			4/10 notices air bubble	4/20 rigid to flexible tubing	4/10 stops flow with hand 4/15 stops flow with cork			
Pipes (with water)	5/5 water comes out opposite where it goes in	5/5 tipping the pipe will stop flow						5/5 suggests using a bucket to catch the water

A.8 Sample Individual Assessment for Science in Art

CHILD: CLAIRE

Activity	hypothesize	predict	observe	compare	experiment	classify	infer	additional comments
Painting with make-up brushes		3/3 blue and yellow make green	9/30 dripping	10/11 thick to thin	12/4 mixes colors		10/20 less paints, less drips	
Glue			9/30 dries clear	4/11 glue to tape	9/10 "paints" glue		1/2 more glue needed for heavy objects	
Double Brush			5/18 makes two marks with only one handle		5/15 holds one brush in each hand			

A.9 Sample Individual Assessment for Science in Music

CHILD: KAREN

Music Center	hypothesize	predict	observe	compare	experiment	classify	infer	additional comments
Triangles (2 sizes)				9/21 compares sound of two sizes	9/19 hits triangles and listens to sound		9/19 triangles of diff. sizes make diff. sounds	
Mallet Medley	11/10 hard beaters sound loud					11/10 beaters that sound soft vs. loud		
Maraca Fillers			12/4 looks at fillers as she shakes maracas	12/7 loudness of sound of 3 fillers	12/4 shakes maracas hard and softly			
Clay Disks (3 sizes)			2/5 disks move when struck				2/9 small objects make high sound	
Water Glasses	5/5 adding water changes the sound			5/8 depth of water and pitch				

More Than Magnets